ITALIAN NEOREALISM

REBUILDING THE CINEMATIC CITY

MARK SHIEL

WALLFLOWER

LONDON and NEW YORK

A Wallflower Paperback

First published in Great Britain in 2006 by
Wallflower Press
6a Middleton Place, Langham Street, London W1W 7TE
www.wallflowerpress.co.uk

A catalogue record for this book is available from the British Library

ISBN 1 904764 48 7

Book Design by Rob Bowden Design

Printed in Great Britain by Antony Rowe Ltd, Chippenham, Wiltshire

£12.99

SHORT CUTS

This book is to be returned on or before the last date stamped below or you will be charged a fine

CONTENTS

ACKNOWLEDGEMENTS

In researching and writing this book, I have benefited greatly from the wisdom and advice of Geoffrey Nowell-Smith, of Queen Mary, University of London, and Chris Wagstaff, of the University of Reading. Both read drafts of the manuscript and responded with thoughtful insights and positive criticisms which allowed me to fine-tune my argument and interpretations. Thomas Hines, of the School of Architecture, University of California, Los Angeles, applied his expertise to reading and commenting on sections of the manuscript pertaining to the Italian city and its architecture. Nicholas Watkins, of the University of Leicester, shared his thoughts with me and, very kindly, a draft copy of some of his recent writing on the issue of fascism and the monument. Additionally, I have greatly appreciated discussions about cinematic time and Rossellini with Laura Mulvey, at Birkbeck College, and about Antonioni with Peter Wollen, at UCLA. Vincent Guigeno and André Gunthert, at the Institut national d'histoire de l'art, Paris, and Reinhold Viehoff, of Martin-Luther-Universität, Halle-Wittenberg, invited me to give papers on my work in progress on Antonioni and the city. Yoram Allon at Wallflower Press has been an understanding and efficient editor as the project has taken shape. My father, Diarmuid Shiel, offered opinions and encouragement along the way. Alyce Mahon, my *ossessione*, supported me in more ways than one, and shared some memorable *flânerie* around Rome.

Author's note: titles of films are given in English where the film received a significant English-language release and the English-language title has since become well-established in film scholarship. All such films are given with their original title in parentheses on their first citation in the text. Otherwise films are given their original titles only.

Mark Shiel
King's College, University of London
January 2006

INTRODUCTION: DESCRIBING NEOREALISM

Few moments in the history of cinema have been as hotly debated in their day and by succeeding generations as the moment of Italian neorealism in Italy after World War Two. Most critics and historians agree that neorealism was a watershed in which realism emerged for a time as the dominant mode of Italian cinema, with decisive impacts on the ways in which films would be made and thought about in Italy and worldwide for generations. One of the most important ways of thinking about neorealism has been to see it as a moment of decisive transition in the tumultuous aftermath of world war which produced a stylistically and philosophically distinctive cinema that achieved a limited but influential popularity from the mid-1940s until some time in the early or late 1950s, depending on the flexibility with which one uses the term: for example, from Roberto Rossellini's *Rome, Open City* (*Roma, città aperta*, 1945) to Vittorio De Sica's *Umberto D* (1952), or from Luchino Visconti's *Ossessione* (1943) to Federico Fellini's *The Nights of Cabiria* (*Le notti di Cabiria*, 1957). In particular, neorealism marked a significant stage in the transformation of cinema from the classical forms which dominated in Europe and in the US prior to World War Two to the modernist art cinemas which came to dominate in Europe after the war and which had considerable impact and influence on Hollywood too from the 1950s to the 1970s.

Neorealism is also often thought of not so much as a particular moment, defined by starting and ending dates, but as a historically- and culturally-specific manifestation of the general aesthetic quality known as 'realism' which is characterised by a disposition to the ontological truth of the physical, visible world. From this perspective, the realism of Italian neorealism manifested itself in a distinctive visual style. This was typified by a preference for location filming, the use of nonprofessional actors, the avoidance of ornamental *mise-en-scène*, a preference for natural light, a freely-moving documentary style of photography, a non-interventionist approach to film directing, and an avoidance of complex editing and other post-production processes likely to focus attention on the contrivance of the film image. Not all neorealist films employed *all* of these strategies, especially in the 1950s when neorealism became increasingly concerned with subjective experience, but most of these strategies are evident in all neorealist films. The perception of neorealism as visual truth is closely identified with the influential critical position of André Bazin who, more than any other non-Italian, argued in favor of neorealism as a cinematic agenda, thinking of it as a cinema of 'fact' and 'reconstituted reportage' (1971a: 20, 37).

The sense of neorealism as visual truth coincides and sometimes clashes with another sense of neorealism as a sentiment of ethical and political commitment – a social realism which motivated not only film-makers but writers such as Elio Vittorini and Italo Calvino, painters such as Renato Guttuso and Aldo Borgonzoni, photographers such as Mario De Biasi and Federico Patellani and, as we shall see in chapter three, architects such as Ludovico Quaroni and Mario Ridolfi. Neorealist cinema has often been characterised as what Mira Liehm calls 'an aesthetics of rejection' (1984: 132) in which the visual style, mythology, politics and working methods of fascist-era cinema were thrown out. In their place, neorealist filmmakers demonstrated a commitment through visual realism to making known the lot of ordinary, everyday Italians, especially the working class. They were inspired by leftist politics, especially the agendas of the Italian Communist Party (PCI) and Socialist Party (PSI), and by the determination to create a new and better Italy after the degradation and barbarity of fascism and in spite of the conservative tendencies of the mainstream of Italian political life, represented by the Catholic Church and the Christian Democrat (DC) party. Especially after 1948, the latter was the dominant force in political life.

This sense of neorealism as a political or ethical disposition leads into another – that of neorealism as a more or less coherent movement of particular directors, writers, cinematographers, editors and actors who were loosely connected to each other through personal and professional associations, who shared anti-fascist convictions and a leftist politics, and who produced a recognisable body of work from the mid-1940s to the mid-1950s. Three directors produced most of the generally recognised masterworks of neorealism – Rossellini's *Rome, Open City, Paisà* (1946), and *Germany Year Zero* (*Germania anno zero*, 1947), De Sica's *Shoeshine* (*Sciuscià*, 1946), *Bicycle Thieves* (*Ladri di biciclette*, 1948) and *Umberto D*, and Visconti's *La terra trema* (1948). After these, one must acknowledge key filmmakers who began as writers, making their directorial debuts in the 1950s with films which pushed the boundaries of neorealism as in the cases of Michelangelo Antonioni, who spent the war years as a critic writing prolifically for the noted journal *Cinema* before directing his first feature, *Cronaca di un amore*, in 1950, and Federico Fellini who wrote for the screen in the late 1940s, making decisive contributions to such films as Rossellini's *Paisà* and *The Miracle* (*Il miracolo*, 1948), before co-directing *Variety Lights* (*Luci del varietà*, 1950) with Alberto Lattuada and directing his own first feature *The White Sheik* (*Lo sceicco bianco*, 1952). Other important directors regularly considered as neorealist would include Giuseppe De Santis, Pietro Germi, Carlo Lizzani and Aldo Vergano, while directors whose fidelity to the aesthetics and politics of neorealism is often debated because of the allegedly superficial neorealist style of many of their films include Alberto Lattuada and Luigi Zampa. Many of these knew each other prior to the advent of neorealism: Visconti, Antonioni, De Santis and others such as Mario Alicata and Pietro Ingrao all being associated with the *Cinema* journal during the war. Some formed regular director/writer collaborations – Rossellini and Fellini and, more famously, De Sica and Cesare Zavattini who, more than any other Italian, developed neorealism as a positive and clearly articulated doctrine. Certain actors such as Anna Magnani in *Rome, Open City*, Silvana Mangano in De Santis' *Bitter Rice* (*Riso amaro*, 1949) and Massimo Girotti in Germi's *In the Name of the Law* (*In nome della legge*, 1949), came to be associated with neorealism as icons of the ordinary Italian people and their suffering after the war. Key cinematographers such as G. R. Aldo (*La terra trema*), Otello Martelli (*Paisà*), Carlo Montuori (*Bicycle Thieves*) and Aldo Tonti (*Ossessione*) worked frequently with the key neorealist directors and were responsible for much of neorealism's distinctive visual immediacy.

How many neorealist films these people produced remains a bone of contention. Most critics agree on the seven key works, all produced in the late 1940s – *Rome, Open City*, *Paisà*, *Germany Year Zero*, *Shoeshine*, *Bicycle Thieves*, *Umberto D* and *La terra trema* – but beyond these what constitutes a neorealist film remains a subject of debate. Whether films such as *Miracle in Milan* (*Miracolo a Milano*, 1951), *I vitelloni* (1953), *Journey to Italy* (*Viaggio in Italia*, 1953), *Senso* (1954) or *The Nights of Cabiria* could be described as neorealist at all was hotly disputed when they were released during the seemingly endless so-called 'crisis of neorealism' of the 1950s. As we shall see in subsequent chapters, each of these was seen either to move neorealism into new territory or to break with it altogether, and opinion as to the neorealism of these films remains divided today. Indeed, the diversity of filmmakers and films grouped under the term 'neorealism' has led a number of film historians, including Geoffrey Nowell-Smith, Peter Bondanella and Pierre Sorlin, to question its usefulness. For example, in his influential study *Luchino Visconti*, first published in 1967, Nowell-Smith suggested that 'neorealism' was only a convenient label to describe a 'pattern of brief convergence around a diffuse blob on the film-historical map' (2003: 27) during the four or five years after World War Two. The crucial differences which he identified between Visconti's politically astute but aesthetically stylised realism and Rossellini's deeply moralistic but more purely realist cinema are only the clearest of the many contrasts which existed within neorealism. More recently, Alberto Farassino has characterised a 'permanent neorealism' which coloured and conditioned all Italian filmmaking in the five years after the liberation of Italy and which 'extended well beyond its specific historical moment to constitute a sort of vein, even a "universal" aesthetic category' (1998: 75). But such observations ought not to invalidate a sense of neorealism as a more or less coherent phenomenon. The view which underpins this book is a flexible one which sees neorealism as a complex but nonetheless useful and vital term of description of a relatively coherent but always evolving historical moment and movement in Italian cinema from the mid-1940s to the mid-1950s, which may be used to discuss a variety of filmmakers and films whose stylistic and ideological similarities outweighed their differences. If neorealism was not an *organised* movement, it was nonetheless a movement, and certainly the most prominent in international cinema in the ten years after World War Two, a cinema which displayed more coherence of formal and thematic concerns among Italian filmmakers than was evident at the time in American, French, British, Soviet or any other cinema.

Although neorealist filmmakers did not regularly collaborate to issue manifestoes, a reasonably large body of neorealist theory and criticism did develop: Zavattini's 'Some Ideas on the Cinema' (1952) and other writings; Lizzani's history *Il cinema italiano* (1953), and the innumerable articles, interviews and interventions by critics and filmmakers which proliferated in *Cinema*, *Bianco e nero* and elsewhere. This theory and criticism grew around a body of films which, though substantial, was only ever a minority tendency in Italian cinema: estimates of the number of films which can be described as neorealist vary from Pierre Sorlin's low calculation of just twenty (or four per cent of total production), to Lino Miccichè's estimate of not more than ninety between 1945 and 1953 (out of a total of 822), to David Forgacs' more generous reckoning of 259 (nearly one-third of total production) in the same period (Sorlin 1996: 93; Miccichè 1999: 21; Forgacs 1990: 117). Neorealist films were, even by the most generous estimate, always a minority of the films Italian cinema produced in any given year.

Moreover, neorealist films were not generally commercially and critically successful although, when they were, they were often high-profile in their success and in the public and critical controversies they provoked. *Rome, Open City* was a worldwide critical and commercial success, as were *Paisà*, *In the Name of the Law*, *Bicycle Thieves* and *Bitter Rice*, but most others did not perform well in box-office terms, especially given the quick post-war re-establishment of commercial genre film production in Italy and the return of Hollywood cinema to market dominance. *Rome, Open City* was exceptional in topping the Italian box office in 1945–46 at 162m lire. Many other successful neorealist films were more modest in their commercial performance – for example, *Paisà* was the ninth most successful film in Italy in 1946–47 generating 100m lire at the box office, *Bicycle Thieves* was eleventh in 1948–49 with 252m lire and *Bitter Rice* was fifth at 442m lire in 1949–50 (Spinazzola 1985: 18). Films imported from the US controlled two-thirds to three-quarters of the Italian box office from 1945 to 1950 – for example, holding a 77 per cent market share in 1948 compared to 13 per cent for Italian films and a 63.7 per cent share in 1950 compared to 29.2 per cent for Italian films (Quaglietti 1980: 248; Liehm 1984: 333). This American dominance was secured by agreements between the Italian film industry's main representative body, the Associazione Nazionale Industrie Cinematografiche ed Affine (ANICA), and its Hollywood counterpart, the Motion Picture Export Association.

Neorealism was arguably welcomed abroad, especially in the US and France, more than it was at home, and in Italy (as well as abroad) its appeal tended to be strongest among educated, urban audiences. Even the most popular and accessible neorealists such as Vittorio De Sica encountered real difficulties securing financing for their films: his *Shoeshine* was a major financial disaster despite its very low budget of less than one million lire and despite winning an Academy Award on its US release; De Sica was subsequently forced to fund many films either by borrowing from friends, for *Bicycle Thieves*, or using his own personal funds, for *Miracle in Milan*.

The period in which neorealism flourished was one of intense struggle in which progressive and conservative forces sought to determine the character and future of Italian society, politics, economics and culture, including cinema. Italy found itself in a process of profound self-exploration, adjustment and reorganisation, an experience which it shared with other countries of Western Europe and elsewhere. Within the context of the Cold War which would quickly come to determine so many aspects of life in the years after 1945, this was essentially a struggle between capitalism and liberal democracy, on the one hand, and various forms and combinations of communism, socialism and social democracy, on the other. In Italy, the main parties to this struggle were the Christian Democrats, in the case of the former, and the Communists and Socialists, in the latter case, although the ascendant power of the United States always made its strong preference clear for capitalism and liberal democracy and had a very real presence and influence on Italian life through the Marshall Plan for the economic and infrastructural reconstruction of Europe (1948–52). Inevitably, this struggle also raged in the cinema where Italian neorealism and Hollywood cinema stood as opposite, divergent models of what popular culture should be and how it should relate to its audience – Italian neorealism embodying the idea of culture as critique, seeking a critical awareness alongside ennobling representations of society with a clear contemporary relevance, and Hollywood cinema, at least to its critics, presenting itself as the epitome of entertainment, not necessarily mindless but not particularly political, compliant and not resistant, escapist and not engaged. Though neither neorealism nor Hollywood was as monolithic as such cursory characterisations suggest – for example, Hollywood cinema in the late 1940s experienced the 'subversion' of *film noir* – neorealism may be seen in this sense not just as a moment of transition but as a moment of particularly overt ideological conflict in cinema.

Their clear national identity also marks neorealist films as products of an era when cinema was still thought of largely in terms of discrete national cultures and the relatively limited 'influences' of one country's national cinema upon that of another – as in the close relationship between French and Italian cinema from the 1930s to the 1950s. The notion of 'national cinema' is an important one in the study of film and neorealism remains an archetype of the post-war art cinemas around which the term was originally developed. One of the presumptions of the national cinema approach is that while films make an interesting object of study in themselves, their ultimate utility lies in the ways they produce 'a collective narrative' of a people and a national culture, as Marcia Landy explains in *Italian Film* (2000: xiii). However, as Landy warns, a balance must be struck between approaching Italian national cinema as a unitary phenomenon, the expression of a discrete and stable national culture, and recognising that on close analysis any national culture and any national cinema is bound to reveal itself to be 'eclectic, fragmentary and contradictory' (2000: xiv).

Neither is any national cinema an island. As we shall see later in this chapter, neorealism was strongly influenced by French cinema of the 1930s and Hollywood cinema coloured the consciousness of its filmmakers and audiences. The international acclaim which greeted neorealism was intense in the United States and in France. Italy, in being liberated from fascism in 1943–44, was immediately also more globalised by its occupation by the Allies and the reopening of its culture, economy and political life to outside influences after the relative isolation of the fascist era. In this circumstance, a new internationalist excitement was part of the cultural atmosphere of the day and provided a liberating light in which filmmakers, critics and audiences were naturally eager to view their film culture. The many non-Italian critics and audiences who welcomed neorealism found that it related profoundly to the war which they too had experienced. Reviewing *Rome, Open City* in the *New York Times* in February 1946, Bosley Crowther wrote:

> It may seem peculiarly ironic that the first film yet seen hereabouts to dramatise the nature and the spirit of underground resistance in German-held Europe in a superior way – with candid, overpowering realism and with a passionate sense of human fortitude – should be a film made in Italy. Yet such is the extraordinary case. *Open City*, which arrived at the World last night, is unquestionably one of the strongest dramatic films yet made about the recent war. And the fact that it was hurriedly put together by a group of artists soon after the liberation of Rome is significant of its fervour and doubtless integrity. (1946: 32)

It was clear that with neorealism Italy experienced a more creative cinematic rebirth after the war than any other combatant nation in World War Two. As P. Adams Sitney has argued, although great films were also made elsewhere, post-war Italian films were superior on the whole to their US, French and British contemporaries in 'their stylistic organisation of elements of apparent rawness, their emotional intensity, and their focus on current political and social problems' (1995: 6). The late 1940s therefore came to constitute what Sitney, drawing on Pier Paolo Pasolini, calls the first of the 'vital crises' which punctuated post-war Italian cinema history, the second being the art cinema of the early 1960s, including Fellini's *La dolce vita* (1960), Pasolini's *Accattone* (1961), Antonioni's *Red Desert* (*Deserto rosso*, 1964), and Bertolucci's *Prima della rivoluzione* (*Before the Revolution*, 1964). The neorealist crisis, artistic and political in roughly equal measure, produced a 'concentration of creative energy' (Sitney 1995: 219) quite peculiar in the history of the medium which appeared to promise profound social and cultural regeneration but which did not necessarily deliver. As Pasolini used the term to look back on neorealism from the 1960s, the notion of a vital crisis was meant not only to convey neorealism's exciting creativity but also its failed opportunities, especially the failure to produce an Italy after the war which was substantially better than that before the war:

> It is useless to delude oneself about it: neorealism was not a regeneration; it was only a vital crisis, however excessively optimistic and enthusiastic at the beginning. Thus poetic action outran thought, formal renewal preceded the reorganisation of the culture through its vitality (let's not forget the year '45!). Now the sudden withering of neorealism is the necessary fate of an improvised, although necessary, superstructure: it is the price for a lack of mature thought, of a complete reorganisation of the culture. (1965: 231)

For Pasolini, as for many others of the neorealist generation and their 1960s descendants, the end of the war, after a brief moment in which everything seemed possible, soon saw a disappointing return to power of Italian capitalism and the Catholic Church, but now backed by the silent partnership of the United States.

In the immediate post-war environment, however, this eventual return to old ways was not predictable and the emphasis for filmmakers, critics and audiences was on the new-ness of the Italian situation after the fall of fascism. Early uses of the term 'neorealism' therefore carried not only a sense of neorealist cinema as something different but as something artistically and morally better than what had gone before. Although the term was occasionally used in the 1930s in relation to literature and Soviet cinema, its popularisation in the context of Italian cinema is often dated from one of two instances: the description in 1943 by Mario Serandrei, the

editor of Visconti's *Ossessione*, of the striking immediacy and freshness of
the imagery he was viewing in the rushes of Visconti's film; or the expression in the same year by the film critic, Umberto Barbaro, of his admiration
for the films of French directors René Clair, Jean Renoir and Marcel Carné,
all of whom were influential on neorealist cinema (see Brunetta 2001:
201–3).

After the war, the term quickly gained currency. Filmmakers, critics
and the cinemagoing public came to a consensus that neorealism arose
out of the trauma of fascism, war and occupation, in response to which it
offered a means of national and personal self-examination. Vittorio De Sica
explained the original impetus for neorealism as 'an overwhelming desire
to throw out of the window the old stories of the Italian cinema, to place the
camera into the mainstream of real life, of everything that struck our horri-
fied eyes' (quoted in Liehm 1984: 59). Luigi Chiarini compared the revela-
tory impact of neorealism to that of the early motion pictures although now
the world 'did not reveal itself in its pleasant exterior, but in its deepest
human content, in the dialectic between war and peace, civilisation and
barbarism, reaction and progress: mechanical reproduction had become
artistic representation' (1979: 145). This sense of neorealism was central to
influential histories of Italian cinema such as Lizzani's *Il cinema italiano*,
and to the writings and teachings of influential critics and educators such
as Barbaro and Guido Aristarco. It also informed the enthusiastic reception
of neorealist films abroad, especially in the United States and in France
where the consensus was strengthened by the critical interventions of
André Bazin and the journal *Cahiers du cinéma*. For Bazin, the most famous
critic to develop a theory of neorealism and to promote its application in
cinema, the term was a valid one despite the frequent impatience of film
directors with what seemed, from their point of view, an abstract category,
and despite the diverse range of films to which the term was applied,
whether a statement of moral outrage such as *Rome, Open City*, a Marxist
analysis of class-based society such as *La terra trema*, a philosophical
enquiry such as *Journey to Italy*, or a historical epic such as *Senso*. For
Bazin, neorealism constituted 'a triumphant evolution of the language of
cinema' (1971a: 26) where, by 'triumphant' Bazin meant not that neorealism was or would eclipse all other forms of cinema but that in its realism it
was more wonderful, more inspiring, than anything else in its day.

Today we can acknowledge Bazin's useful recognition of the innovation
of neorealism without necessarily sharing his faith in the utopian potential of realism as an aesthetic strategy, a faith for which he has received

his share of criticism since the 1940s (see Aumont *et al.* 1999: 108–14). Neorealism did make certain important filmmaking approaches more common in post-war cinema and did give them new legitimacy, even if, as much recent scholarship has shown, some of what the neorealists became most famous for was not unknown in cinema of the fascist era and earlier. For example, one of neorealism's most important and influential areas of innovation was its removal of filmmaking from the confines of the studio to the expanses of the countryside and the built space of the city where the camera could fully engage with physical and social reality. In 1945, this removal had both a material and an ideological impetus behind it. Like those of other countries, especially Germany, Italy's film studios and most of its film equipment were out of commission. In Rome, for example, much equipment from the main studios, Cinecittà, had been removed by the Germans and Italian fascists when they fled the advancing Allies in the late summer of 1943. Filmmakers were forced to look for creative solutions to the problem of producing cinema in conditions of extreme austerity. At the same time, austerity was a characteristic of society as a whole: the brute realities of hunger, poverty, displacement and unemployment with which so many Italians lived imbued the making of cinema with a peculiar moral urgency and social purpose. As Alberto Lattuada explained with more than a hint of nostalgia in 1959:

> After the last war, especially in Italy, it was this very need for reality which forced us out of the studios. It is true that our studios were partly destroyed or occupied by refugees, but it is equally true that the decision to shoot everything on location was above all dictated by the desire to express life in its most convincing manner and with the harshness of documentaries. The very spirit of walls corroded by time and full of the tired signs of history, took on an aesthetic consistency. The actors' costumes were those of the man in the street. Actresses became women again, for a moment. It was a poor but strong cinema, with many things to say in a hurry and in a loud voice, without hypocrisy, in a brief vacation from censorship; and it was an unprejudiced cinema, personal and not industrial, a cinema full of real faith in the language of film, as a means of education and social progress. (Quoted in Armes 1971: 66–7)

Without established sources of financing, the first neorealist films were made with very low budgets and with a minimum of production funds secured in advance by filmmakers for whom location filming helped to reduce costs while also encouraging socially-committed cinema. In the name of authenticity, a film was more often than not filmed where it was set – Aldo Vergano's *Il sole sorge ancora* (1946) in rural Lombardy, Visconti's *La terra trema* in Aci Trezza in Sicily, Rossellini's *Stromboli* (1950) on the volcanic island of that name in the Mediterranean. Sometimes, where a film was based on real-life events, specific streets and buildings used by the film's real-life subjects were used as locations for reproducing their lives, as was the case with Rossellini's filming in the Via Casilina and the Piazza di Spagna in Rome for *Rome, Open City*. On the other hand, *Rome, Open City* contained many indoor sequences filmed in a makeshift studio which Rossellini put together in the Via degli Avignonesi, and in his *Paisà* stand-in locations were used in the episode set in a monastery in the Apennines between Florence and Bologna which was actually filmed at Maiori on the Amalfi coast. Occasionally, such cases would prompt criticism – André Bazin expressed dissatisfaction with the 'melodramatic indulgence' (1971a: 61) of De Sica's use of a studio set to recreate Rome's Porta Portese prison in *Shoeshine* – but they could usually be tolerated if the general principles of authenticity and verisimilitude were not surrendered. Location filming remained the preference of neorealist directors through the mid-1950s and beyond. It was accompanied by a cinematography which aspired to documentary-like objectivity and austerity, a preference for long- and medium-shots in deep-focus, an avoidance of unnatural camera movements or camera angles (including close-ups) and a favouring of natural light over what Bazin condemned as the 'plastic compositions' (1971a: 65) of studio lighting. It was reinforced by editing which sought to minimise the manipulation of time and space by cutting as little as possible and by aiming towards a cinematic equivalent of real-time in which, according to Bazin, every shot 'must now respect the actual duration of the event' (ibid.).

These characteristics have long underpinned the recognition of neorealism as a particularly visual form of cinema which Angela Dalle Vacche has contextualised within the larger tendency of Italian culture as a whole to downplay the verbal and the written (1992: 5). This tendency is demonstrated in the neorealist practice of dubbing the soundtrack in post-production and in the deprioritisation of elements such as script, dialogue and literary sources which are central to other cinemas, especially Hollywood. Because the dubbing of films had been compulsory under the fascist regime, most neorealist films were shot without sound and all dialogue was added to the image track after the fact. This had an anti-realist effect in dislocating the original sound and image but, as in the case of *Rome, Open City*, Italian filmmakers had become quite expert in the technique by the 1940s and, in most cases, any loss of realism due to dubbing was compensated for by the distinctive mobility and expanded field of view which relatively lightweight silent film cameras afforded the cinematographer.

Neorealist films therefore distinguished themselves in their interest in the visualisation of the ordinary events and environments of Italian life. Of course, most neorealist films, including those such as *Bicycle Thieves* for whom chance itself was a major theme, were underpinned by some classical narrative structure, following a line from initial stasis to exposition to struggle and resolution, but doing so without the dramatic urgency or storytelling efficiency of classical cinema, especially classical Hollywood, and in films such as *Paisà* or *Umberto D* neorealism came close to dispensing with classical structure altogether. Both of these films contained a high degree of what David Bordwell has called 'narrative irresolution' (1993: 209) in so far as they resisted logically and emotionally satisfying narrative closure. Instead, neorealist films tended to focus on open-ended situations, especially the fleeting moments of encounter between human beings or between human beings and their environment which led the German film historian Siegfried Kracauer to cherish neorealism for its revelation of the disjointed, haphazard and chance-based 'flow' (1997: 31) of modern life. This was partly the result of neorealism's relative de-prioritisation of literary sources and of the script. Although works of contemporary Italian literature such as Elio Vittorini's *Uomini e no* (*Men and Not Men*, 1945), Italo Calvino's *Il sentiero dei nidi di ragno* (*The Path to the Nest of Spiders*, 1947) and Cesare Pavese's *La luna e i falò* (*The Moon and the Bonfires*, 1950) were frequently described as 'neorealist' because they arose out of the same social and political conditions, and dealt with many of the same themes of post-war, post-fascist Italy, neorealist cinema and literature actually had very little practical interaction. As with Zavattini's adaptation of *Bicycle Thieves* from Luigi Bartolini's novel (1946) or Visconti's adaptation of *La terra trema* from Giovanni Verga's *I Malavoglia* (1881), those scripts which did have literary sources were generally loose in their adaptation. The deprioritisation of narrative and literary sources signified a refusal of loyalty to the written word which was seen to restrict the potential for realism. Neorealist scripts were usually collaboratively produced by several contributors and left significant room for modification during shooting. While Luchino Visconti proposed that a film must always give the 'impression of improvisation' (quoted in Armes: 1971: 187) even if it was not actually improvised, Cesare Zavattini professed a desire to jettison narrative altogether.

By extension, neorealist filmmakers refused to be tied by conventional approaches to acting and performance, instead employing non-professional actors and casting professional actors against type in order to revise the notion of acting as the performance of fictional roles by film stars. For Kracauer, who championed neorealism in his *Theory of Film*, first published in 1960, the playing of the lead roles by non-professionals in De Sica's *Bicycle Thieves* and *Umberto D* produced an admirable 'documentary touch', while their anonymity countered cinematic stardom by focusing the viewer's attention on 'social patterns' rather than 'individual destinies' (1997: 99). In being untrained, performances by non-professionals carried a desirable raw authenticity of physique, behaviour and mannerism. In *La terra trema*, these were central to Visconti's casting of real Sicilian fishermen and villagers in his study of the impoverished community of Aci Trezza, and were underlined by the scripting of the film entirely in local dialect. Meanwhile, where neorealist films did employ professional actors, these were often cast in such a way as to modify their established screen personae and thereby question traditional modes of performance. Massimo Girotti had been a wartime heart-throb in the romance *A Romantic Adventure* (*Una romantica avventura*, 1940) and the mythological epic *La Corona di ferro* (1941) before Visconti cast him in *Ossessione*, an anti-establishment drama of murder and adultery with homosexual overtones. Rossellini cast the comic actors Anna Magnani and Aldo Fabrizi in tragic roles in *Rome, Open City*, and argued that, in any case, he was not interested in their stardom but only in the ways in which their peculiarly natural acting style allowed him to 'make contact with humanity' (see Rosselini 1946).

The search for authentic human experience and interaction was a central preoccupation of neorealist cinema from the outset, and, like neorealism's questioning of cinematic stardom, was no doubt partly informed by a reaction against the rhetorical insincerity and inhumanity of the fascist regime and its projection of the political 'stardom' of Mussolini. Against this, and in view of the traumatic experience of war and post-war hardship (both material and psychological), character became a subject in itself. Neorealist films often lacked narrative momentum and the determined heroic protagonist of classical cinema. Neorealist protagonists were often hopelessly oppressed or deeply troubled and often victims of chance or fate which testified to the fragility and contingency of life in the aftermath of war – a stray bullet from a German gun in *Paisà*, the theft of a bicycle in *Bicycle Thieves*. The opportunity for self-exploration and a re-evaluation of Italian society which neorealism provided led to examinations of the nature of human existence on both the social and existential levels, and these levels were always intricately related. Naturally, earlier neorealist films demonstrated a greater concern for the immediate conditions of post-war, post-fascist Italy. Oppression, poverty, crime, unemployment, homelessness, class and power in Italian society were at the centre of all of the most important neorealist films from 1943 to 1948, a period generally identified as the crucible in which neorealism was formed and in which many of the most important films were made. But within this concern with material conditions, there was variation between the preoccupation with morality of Rossellini and De Sica's films and the more political concerns of Visconti, De Santis and Germi. As we shall see in subsequent chapters, material concerns became gradually less central to neorealism, especially in the 1950s when, in an atmosphere of increasing economic stability and even abundance, the emphasis shifted to the question of spiritual rather than material lack. It is for this reason that the 1950s are often seen as a period of 'crisis' for neorealism in which it lost its artistic and ideological coherence and momentum, or even a period in which a fundamental 'break' with neorealism occurred, of which the first signs include Roberto Rossellini's *L'Amore* (1948), Fellini and Lattuada's *Variety Lights*, and Antonioni's *Cronaca di un amore*.

In truth, however, neorealism was always in crisis, even in 1945. This book is structured in such as a way as to recognise an *evolution* in neorealism from the 1940s to the following decade, rather than a break. As will be argued in the following chapters, the formal characteristics of neorealism in the 1950s demonstrated both continuity and change: location filming and loose narrative remained central; non-professional actors were still used, though with decreasing frequency after *Umberto D*; visual austerity prevailed, though certain films such as Visconti's *Senso* seemed to undermine it. Neorealism became increasingly self-conscious, giving way to a modernist experimentation increasingly skeptical of the truth of images of 'the real' and tending toward greater degrees of abstraction and interiorised philosophical enquiry. As will be suggested in chapter five, perhaps no single film epitomised this tendency more than Fellini's *The Nights of Cabiria*.

Metaphysical issues of morality, interpersonal communication, guilt and responsibility were prominent in Rossellini's immediately post-war films and were further examined, albeit with greater and greater degrees of formal experimentation, in his films of the 1950s: *Francis, God's Jester* (*Francesco, giullare di Dio*, 1950), *The Machine to Kill Bad People* (*La macchina ammazzacattivi*, 1952), *Europa '51* (1952), and *Journey to Italy*. Most neorealist films focused on contemporary Italy to such an extent that when Visconti's *Senso* emerged in 1954, its historical setting during the mid-nineteenth century emergence of Italy as a nation-state (the period known as the Risorgimento) was taken by many as evidence of a break with neorealism even though *Rome, Open City* and *Paisà* were already historical films in a broad sense, if set in the much more recent past. Similarly the evolution of the work of De Sica and Zavattini after *Bicycle Thieves* is one of continuity despite the elements of fantasy which are worked into the neorealism of *Miracle in Milan* and the return to an extremely austere form of neorealism immediately afterwards in *Umberto D*. In other words, what began immediately after the war as a way of thinking about the war and its material, psychic and social consequences gradually evolved into a way of thinking about the material, psychic and social character of peacetime society, especially in relation to urban modernity which became the default mode of existence for more and more Italians as the 1950s progressed.

As will be argued throughout this book, one of the most important continuous concerns of neorealist cinema was with the city and with the processes of modernisation – for example, post-war reconstruction, industrialisation, secularisation and rural-to-urban migration – of which the city was the clearest expression. On the one hand, the numerous neorealist films set in rural Italy present a range of spaces from near-wilderness (*Stromboli*) to agricultural community (*Bitter Rice*) to the small town (*In the Name of the Law*) in which each type of space bears a distinctive relationship of proximity to or remoteness from the modernising processes at play in the nation as a whole. In many such films, the city as such is missing from the *mise-en-scène* but it is present as a 'structuring absence', as an offscreen space to which characters depart or from which they arrive in ways which have decisive effects on rural space and the events which take place within it. On the other hand, the numerous neorealist films set in urban space, from *Rome, Open City* to *The Nights of Cabiria*, anticipate and represent much more directly the modernising processes at the heart of the city which would come to define the fabric of life for a majority of Italians in the decades after World War Two and which would come to connect Italy to the increasingly globalised economic and cultural realities of the post-war era. As will be suggested throughout the book, but especially in chapter three, neorealist films set in urban space, precisely because of

their urban settings, would speak more powerfully than their rural counterparts to the Italian and international experience of war as a cataclysm
of physical destruction and rebuilding – a cataclysm which could not
fail to achieve more convincing and resonant form in densely-built and
populated urban spaces than in the immutable and timeless spaces of
the countryside. Indeed, in a sense the war itself, and the fascist agres-
sion which provoked it, had been a product of the failings of a new kind of
urban industrial modernity which had emerged in Europe in the nineteenth
century. Neorealist films set in urban space were deeply preoccupied with
the iconography, social make-up, phenomenological experience and widespread influence of the city: as a physical space with distinctive sights and
sounds; as a lived environment in which the struggle for food or work was
particularly intense; as a mental concept supposedly signifying human
achievement and progress but, often in neorealist films, represented by
little more than wastelands and ruins; and, with Italy's gradual economic
recovery after the war, as an engine of modernisation whose economic
power and infrastructural networks reached ever deeper into the rural hin-
terland through both overt and subliminal forms of urbanisation.

Therefore, the organisation of ideas in this book as a whole, and the
selection of six films for close analysis – *Ossessione, Rome, Open City,
Bicycle Thieves, Cronaca di un amore, Journey to Italy* and *The Nights of
Cabiria* – reflects the conviction that an understanding of the Italian city,
urbanisation and its representation is the key to the understanding of
neorealism. In the following chapters we shall attempt to trace a history of
neorealism in which urban images are never far from view while proposing
that the historical evolution of neorealism in cinema, and of the utopian
hopes, intellectual debates and political controversies which surrounded
it, is tellingly reflected in the history of the post-war Italian city.

1   THE ORIGINS OF NEOREALISM

Influences on neorealism

Italian neorealism has always been both an Italian and an international phenomenon and neorealist films and filmmakers regularly drew on both Italian and foreign influences. The neorealist filmmakers of the 1940s and 1950s were among the most well-schooled in film history, capitalising on the proliferation of popular film culture and of film education in Italy during the 1930s, and drawing upon a wide range of cinematic precedents. In respect of neorealism's documentary-like preoccupation with the everyday life of a society, the Soviet montage school of the 1920s was not widely known but had a specialised influence, especially through the translation of Russian film theory by Umberto Barbaro and the teaching of Russian filmmaking techniques at the national film school, the Centro Sperimentale di Cinematografia (see Brunetta 2001: 167–74). More influential because they were more thoroughly part of the common culture were French cinema, especially the poetic realism of Jean Renoir and Marcel Carné, which enjoyed commercial success in Italy and provided some of the most important neorealist filmmakers with their first experiences of filmmaking, and Hollywood cinema, which, prior to its exclusion by the fascist authorities in 1938, enjoyed widespread popularity and a dominant position in the market.

Of all influences on neorealist cinema, none was more important than that of French cinema – especially the work of Renoir, Carné and René Clair, which was popular with Italian audiences in the 1930s and became even more so after 1938 when Hollywood films were no longer available in Italy.

The aesthetics and ethics of their films were regularly cited as an inspiration for the rejuvenation of Italian cinema called for by Giuseppe De Santis, Mario Alicata, Antonio Pietrangeli and Umberto Barbaro in their critical writings for *Cinema* and *Bianco e nero* in the early 1940s (see Quaresima 1996). The French film industry provided important professional opportunities to neorealist filmmakers in their days as young apprentices to major French directors. De Sica and Rossellini readily acknowledged their admiration of the films of Clair, and Antonioni worked as an assistant on Carné's *Les visiteurs du soir* (1942). Visconti spent much of his early adulthood in France, gained his first professional experience working as an assistant to Renoir on *Une partie de campagne* (1936), and regularly cited the influence of 1930s French poetic realism on his own later work in cinema. Renoir's *Toni* (1935) provided a precursor of neorealism in its focus on working-class subjects, its downplaying of stardom and glamour and its location filming in the French provinces while Visconti's first feature, *Ossessione* – generally recognised as the most important Italian forerunner of neorealism, if not itself the first neorealist film proper – drew heavily on the admiration for French cinema which Visconti shared with the film's scriptwriter, Giuseppe De Santis.

Only American culture had a more widespread presence in Italy before World War Two. Italians cultivated a fascination with the United States due to America's status as a popular icon of urban modernity and Italy's important emigrant population in the US whose letters and remittances sent home to family in the old country were inspiring points of contact between continents. Italian appreciation of American cinema was widespread. The neorealists admired Hollywood directors from William Wyler and Frank Capra to John Ford and King Vidor, both realist and epic in their cinematic visions. In the 1930s, Italian audiences were drawn to the realism and modernity of the American gangster film, and to escapist American movies, including those of popular icons such as Mickey Mouse, and Disney's *Snow White and the Seven Dwarfs* (1937). According to Pierre Sorlin, during the period 1930 to 1935, US films accounted for sixty to seventy per cent of total box-office revenue in Italy while Italian films amounted to a relatively small 15–17 per cent (1996: 56). Faced with this reality, the fascist regime was ambivalent. At the end of the 1920s, the playwright Luigi Pirandello, a fascist sympathiser, declared his hostility to the coming of sound cinema as the manifestation of a vulgar American popular culture which was antithetical to theatre and art. Mussolini, however, pragmatically tolerated the prominence of Hollywood, at least partly in recognition of the Italian emigrant connection. But that tolerance would run out in 1938 when, under the new doctrine of national self-sufficiency known as 'autarchy', the regime unilaterally assumed responsibility for the distribution of all imported films, effectively freezing the Hollywood studios and their films out of Italy until 1944. For James Hay, the 'essentialism and imperialism' (1987: 66) which dominated Italian political life in the 1920s and 1930s can be seen, in part, as a reaction to Americanisation among conservative groups in Italian society.

For many Italian writers, meanwhile, American culture provided a surrogate culture of resistance to fascism. Writers such as Alberto Moravia, Cesare Pavese and Elio Vittorini favored American authors of realist or naturalist leanings such as Sinclair Lewis, Theodor Dreiser, John Steinbeck, William Faulkner and John Dos Passos. Moravia translated Ernest Hemingway and others into Italian, and James M. Cain's *The Postman Always Rings Twice* (1934) was adapted by De Santis and Visconti to become the film *Ossessione* in 1943, though the book itself was not published in Italian until 1945. This socially-oriented literature, much of it compiled in Vittorini's influential anthology, *Americana* (1941), remained popular in Italy despite the restrictive cultural and political climate of the fascist regime. American literature grated against the ultra-nationalism of official literary figures such as Gabriele D'Annunzio (1863–1938), the writer and soldier whose Nietzschean romanticism, super-masculine iconography and virulent anti-liberal, anti-communist politics were beloved of the fascists. This is not to say that America was idealised – rather it was seen, as Pavese put it, as 'a sort of great laboratory' (quoted in Liehm 1984: 36) which exemplified the latest political, cultural, economic and social trends in modern urban society in a way which was exciting if also somewhat disturbing. In 1935, Mario Soldati became one of the most important commentators on the ambivalent myth of America through his book *America primo amore* (*America: First Love*, 1935), which provided a detailed account of his experiences of the energy and diversity of American culture and society during two years he spent working and completing a fellowship at Columbia University in New York. In his characterisation, the United States functioned as a symbolic counterweight to the dominant nationalist mythology and imposed social order of the fascist era.

But if American literature and, to a certain extent, American film provided a realist counter to the mythologising tendencies of fascism, realist tendencies had been established in Italy much earlier. Indeed, Italy can be said to have been the birthplace of the realist representation which dominated Western art, in the sense of perspective and figuration, from the Renaissance to the early twentieth century. Italian cinema, from its earliest days, was constituted by a tension between a dominant spectacular and a minor realist tendency which Angela Dalle Vacche has explained in terms of the opposing Italian cultural traditions of opera and of the *commedia dell'arte* – the former heroic, legendary and statuesque, and the latter, like neorealism, concerned with small-scale realities, and human, everyday interactions and environments (1992: 3–5). The dominant tendency of Italian cinema prior to the advent of the fascists in 1922 was towards technically-sophisticated and lavish melodrama and historical epic of the type provided by films from *The Taking of Rome* (director unknown, 1905), *The Fall of Troy* (*La caduta di Troia*, 1910) and *Agnes Visconti* (1910) to *Cabiria* (1912) and *Quo Vadis?* (1914). But this tendency was met by an important, if minor, strain of documentary-style realism which flourished in *Assunta Spina* (1915) and *Sperduti nel buio* (1914) as well as in the films of Elvira Notari, *A santa notte* and *È piccerella* (both 1922), which were often filmed on location with non-professional actors in working-class environments and which achieved critical recognition after World War Two when Italian and French film historians such as Umberto Barbaro and Georges Sadoul pointed to them as important antecedents of neorealism.

However, while signs of early Italian cinema, as well as French and American film and literature, could be seen throughout neorealism, nothing influenced it more deeply than the social and political regime of fascism from which it emerged and against which it was formed, both ideologically and artistically.

Italian cinema under fascism

From its inception in 1922 until the end of that decade, the fascist regime was only remotely involved in the Italian film industry, assuming that film production was best handled by private interests seeking to emulate the commercially-oriented entertainment model of Hollywood. However, this approach proved unsustainable. From a dominant position in international cinema prior to World War One, competition from Hollywood, France and Germany increased, production companies and Italy's famous star system (*divismo*) became unprofitable, the industry fell behind international standards in equipment and training, and Italian films lost foreign market share, especially with the coming of sound. Overall feature film production fell from 371 films in 1920 to 8 in 1930. Studios in Milan and Turin were abandoned, production in Naples declined, and Rome remained the only area of continuing feature production, mostly carried out by small, independent companies (see Sorlin 1996: 53). With the exception of Italy's one major film distributor-exhibitor, Stefano Pittaluga, and the studio Cines, Italy's feature film industry was in dire straits.

However, the fascist regime had quickly realised the usefulness of documentary film in building and maintaining political power. In 1926, it had founded L'Unione Cinematografica Educativa (LUCE) which produced large volumes of documentaries and newsreels emphasising Italy's economic, industrial and cultural progress and making the image of Mussolini ubiquitous in Italian society. In 1929, when the regime consolidated its power by declaring Italy a one-party state, it launched the Ente nazionale per la cinematografia to give greater coordination to the film industry in response to its economic crisis and to provide Italy with a vibrant and modern film industry to rival those of other great powers. Subsequently, the fascist regime developed a sophisticated carrot-and-stick set of initiatives to foster Italian film production and then dramatically increased its control of the industry after 1936 just as it commenced its imperial wars in Africa and the Balkans, intervened in the Spanish Civil War on Franco's side, initiated the policy of economic and cultural autarchy, and formalised its long-standing alliance with Nazism. The desirability of fascist influence on all aspects of film culture, not just documentary, became clear and cinema was recognised by Mussolini as 'the most powerful weapon'. The regime's approach to film culture was to foster the production and consumption of Italian films within ideological and industrial parameters which, although not as rigorous as those applied by the Nazi regime to German cinema, were nonetheless carefully-controlled and consonant with its agenda.

In 1932, the Mostra cinematografica di Venezia was inaugurated as an extension of the Venice Arts Festival, giving official cultural credibility to the medium. From 1933, Fascist party cinema youth clubs, the so-called Cine-GUF (Gioventù universitaria fascista), promoted film among the proliferating educated middle-class youth population. The founding of the Centro Sperimentale di Cinematografia in 1935, led by Luigi Chiarini, provided Italy with one of the world's most sophisticated film schools where students, including the future neorealists Rossellini, Antonioni, De Santis, Zampa and Germi, were exposed to the influences of Eisenstein, Pudovkin, Arnheim and Balázs and to new critical debates about film. Italy's increasingly intellectual film culture was epitomised by the Centro's theoretically-oriented in-house journal *Bianco e Nero* (founded in 1937) and by *Cinema* (founded in 1936) which, despite being edited from 1938 by Vittorio Mussolini, provided young film critics, including Antonioni and De Santis, with early opportunities to publish their ideas. *Cinema* soon became known for its belief that cinema should display a commitment to the subject of contemporary Italian society and to the naturalistic aesthetic of *verismo*. As a new generation of filmmakers and critics was produced, feature-film production was also significantly boosted by the establishment of the state-of-the-art and state-funded Cinecittà studios, on the Via Tuscolana in Rome, which were opened to great fanfare by Mussolini in 1937 and presented as an Italian emulation of the Hollywood model and the epitome of Italy's dynamic urban modernity.

Meanwhile, other initiatives were undertaken which were more clearly aimed at controlling the character of Italian feature films. The Direzione Generale per la Cinematografia was founded in 1933 under Luigi Freddi, himself a fascist and adviser to the regime on cinema, who combined his experiences of visiting Hollywood with the advice of established filmmakers such as Mario Camerini, Alessandro Blasetti and Mario Soldati. Through the Direzione, steps were taken to limit the exhibition of foreign films by imposing taxes on their importation which could be channeled into domestic production, and requiring the dubbing of all foreign films into Italian, while selectively banning certain films, such as Jean Renoir's pacifist film *La Grande illusion* (1937), and funding others according to an official agenda, such as Carmine Gallone's militaristic Roman epic *Scipio Africanus* (1937). This kind of control was extended in 1935 with the Ente Nazionale Industrie Cinematografiche (ENIC) which, thirteen years after the start of the fascist regime, established complete fascist control of the film industry. ENIC controlled all first-run film theatres (*prima visione*) in Italian cities, thereby accounting for eighty per cent of the total box office, and, despite the protests of exhibitors, took over all distribution of foreign films from the private sector in a move which forced the American studios Fox, Paramount, MGM and Warner Bros. to pull out of the Italian market by 1938. Cinema had become central to Italian fascism's political, economic and cultural agendas and its promotion of conservative social values. These values coincided with those of the Catholic Church, which arrived at an accommodation with the fascist regime in the 1929 Lateran Pact and which also sought to promote a patriarchal and sexually-conservative social order, including by means of its own network of cinemas which showed films approved by the Catholic Centre for Cinema (Centro Cattolico Cinematografico) and publicised in its own film magazine *Cinematic*

Information. Following these developments, film production in Italy rose substantially from ten to twenty films per year in the early 1930s to nearly 100 per year in the early 1940s (see Quaglietti 1980: 245). An extensive programme of new cinema building was commenced, cinema audiences grew dramatically, and spending on cinemagoing as a proportion of overall consumer spending on entertainment rose, especially when the government fixed the price of cinema tickets against inflation.

The efforts of the fascist regime to influence the character of Italian feature-film production, distribution and exhibition transformed the Italian film industry into the fifth largest in the world by 1942. They fostered a cinema which was diverse in its formal strategies and thematic concerns but whose diversity was, for the most part, safely contained within ideological confines suitable to the regime. Historical epics and war films were the minority but were generally propagandistic in reinforcing the principles of national superiority, militarism and male heroism and female subservience which underpinned fascism. The most well-known film of this type, *Scipio Africanus*, epitomised the big-budget spectacular, overrun with excessively rhetorical and ornamental representations of classical architecture, costume and the Roman people as symbolic mass. Produced in the aftermath of Italy's invasion and conquest of Ethopia in 1935, the film's publicity proposed that it was intended 'through a distant parallel of events and ideals' to express 'a fate through which after more than two thousand years Africa once again becomes the key of a new Mediterranean and Latin empire' (quoted in Aristarco 1996: 80). Contemporary newsreels associated Mussolini with the film in the public mind through the visits he made to the production during filming. *Scipio Africanus* was funded by the government with the largest budget to that date of any Italian film and it achieved huge box-office success. Its bombast was replicated in other war films with a contemporary setting, such as Augusto Genina's *The White Squadron* (*Lo squadrone bianco*, 1936) which glorified Italian colonialism in Libya through an orientalising representation of the desert landscape and through the heroic figure of the Italian officer, Captain Santelia. The film won the Mussolini Prize for Best Italian Film at Venice in 1936. Goffredo Alessandrini's *Luciano Serra pilota* (1938), part-scripted by a young Roberto Rossellini and produced by Vittorio Mussolini, likewise honoured the heroism of Italian air force pilots in combat in Africa.

Meanwhile, the films of Alessandro Blasetti, who had been instrumental in pushing for a rejuvenated film industry in the 1920s and would remain one of the most important figures in Italian cinema after World War Two, took

23

a direction which was less aggressively rhetorical in style and more subtle in technique. A radical fascist and a filmmaker whose work was admired by Mussolini himself, Blasetti achieved critical success with the silent film *Sole* (1929) which presented a government-run land reclamation project for public housing at the Pontine marshes as evidence of fascism's positive modernising agenda. Much of *Sole* was filmed on location and Blasetti would become known as one of those filmmakers who employed realism as an aesthetic strategy in feature films in ways which contrasted with the artifice of *Scipio Africanus*. His masterpiece, *1860* (1934), presented the drama of Garibaldi's invasion of Sicily and the march of the one thousand which led to the formation of Italy during the Risorgimento. Though the film was a historical epic, it presented history through the extensive use of location filming, non-professional actors speaking in local dialect and scenes of peasant life and rural landscape, characteristics which some historians have taken as anticipating aspects of neorealist filmmaking practice in the post-war period. But its realism was compromised by the heroic battle sequences which made up much of its action, its valorisation of a combative form of Italian patriotism, and its closing sequence which presented contemporary fascists and veterans of the Garibaldi campaign parading together in the Foro Mussolini. Blasetti's enlistment of realism in the fascist cause was also evident in *The Old Guard* (*Vecchia guardia*, 1935), whose drama commences just before Mussolini's 1922 march on Rome and revolves around skirmishes in a small town between local fascists and communists, the former presented as heroes and the latter as brutal thugs. *The Old Guard*, which was one of Hitler's favourite films, became the most infamous of a subgenre in the mid-1930s, including Giovacchino Forzano's *Black Shirt* (*Camicia nera*, 1933) and Giorgio Simonelli's *Dawn over the Sea* (*Aurora sul mare*, 1935), which strategically employed cinematic realism for its tendency to lend authenticity and truthfulness to its characters and subjects, but as a means of legitimising fascism.

Although Blasetti's films tempered the martial rhetoric of the most overtly propagandistic historical epics and war films by emphasising the everyday life of working people in contemporary Italy, they nonetheless wore their fascist politics on their sleeve. As such, they constituted a minority tendency in Italian cinema, but one with a particular symbolic significance and rhetorical presence. Numerically, Italian feature-film production was dominated by escapist genres – costume dramas, musicals, melodramas and comedies. These did not explicitly endorse Italian nationalism, Italy's right to an empire, the rejection of parliamentary democracy, or the physical force ideals of fascism – indeed, most of them made no mention of fascism or war at all. However, they were nevertheless complicit with the agendas of the fascist regime. Among the most important were the popular comedies known as 'white telephone' films, the white telephone being a desirable luxury consumer item of the 1930s. Alessandrini's *The Private Secretary* (*La segretaria privata*, 1931), Genina's *Castles in the Air* (*Castelli in aria*, 1939), Max Neufeld's *Mille lire al mese* (1939) and other films of this type were well-made, cinematically stylish, studio-filmed productions, which contained gentle social satire but were very much endeared to the material wealth and comfort of the upper-middle class and their social status, and to the luxury of their own *mise-en-scène*.

The comedies of Mario Camerini meanwhile injected the genre with notes of cinematic realism, at least in visual style – indeed, Camerini was arguably the most important of those filmmakers who demonstrated realist tendencies in the fascist era. His films were generally romantic comedies focusing on sympathetic lower-middle-class characters, often young lovers, and their dreams for self-improvement in modern urban society. From *The Rails* (*Rotaie*, 1929) and *What Rascals Men Are!* (*Gli uomini, che mascalzoni*, 1932) to *I'll Give a Million* (*Darò un millione*, 1935) and *Il Signor Max* (1937), they were firmly contemporary in their representation of modern romance, the world of work and the excitement of the city environment. They contained mild elements of social critique in contrasting their protagonists with the pampered upper-middle class – a theme which, as James Hay has explained, was concentrated around certain social spaces such as the department store and the luxury hotel that symbolised social and economic ambition and the modernity and material abundance of Italy under fascism (1987: 37–40). Their contemporaneity was enhanced by their employment of visual realism in representing the modern Italian city – for example, the striking location filming of Milan in *What Rascals Men Are!* However, although Camerini was not a fascist, his films were ultimately compatible with fascist imperatives. Their mild social critique and elements of visual realism were generally made safe by their comedy and by the conservative endings of their narratives: the ambitious lower-middle-class protagonists recognise that the key to happiness is not the material wealth and social status to which they aspire – happiness is to be found in the acceptance of one's allotted place in society. The romantic union which typically concludes each film endorses the fascist ideal of the nuclear family as bastion of moral and political order, class antagonism is suppressed in favour of the supposed harmony of the fascist 'corporate state', and urban society under fascism is shown to be productive and fulfilling. In other words, realism is shorn of any socially challenging meaning and remains as an aesthetic surface only.

Italian realism in context

This account runs counter to many aspects of the history of pre- and post-war Italian cinema which has developed since the late 1970s in the work of such commentators as Hay as well as Lino Miccichè, Adriano Aprà, Pierre Sorlin, and Peter Bondanella (Hay 1987; Miccichè 1975; Aprà & Pistagnesi 1979; Sorlin 1996; Bondanella 2001). These scholars have usefully challenged the neat orthodoxies which developed around neorealism in the first two decades after the war by which neorealism was viewed as a revolutionary cinema and Italian cinema of the fascist era was dismissed as vulgar propaganda or decadent entertainment. They have pointed to what they see as continuities between pre-war and post-war realism and weaknesses in the cultural hegemony of Italian fascism, and they have forced a revisitation of the difficult moral issues of the era by pointing out that several of the most important neorealist filmmakers – including Rossellini, De Sica, Zavattini, Visconti, Lattuada and Antonioni – were trained or first worked in cinema during the fascist era. However, in doing so they have raised new problematics which threaten to replace the neat orthodoxies of the past with critical errors to which we may be increasingly prone as the fascist era of Italian history retreats further and further into the past. With respect to fascism, they do not convincingly account for the ability of the fascist regime to hold power continuously for twenty years and they downplay the fact that Italian fascism eventually fell not so much as a result of its own internal contradictions but because of decisive military intervention originating outside Italy. With respect to the cinema, they do not properly consider the appearance of realism under Italian fascism within its full historical and international context, a context to which it is worth devoting some attention at this point because it reminds us to maintain a distinction between conservative and progressive forms of realism which, as an aesthetic strategy, exists *only* in historically and geographically specific cultural forms and types of cinema.

As Colin MacCabe explained in his 1974 essay, 'Realism and the Cinema: Notes on Some Brechtian Theses', the significance of realism as an aesthetic strategy shifted markedly through the nineteenth and twentieth centuries in literature and film. In the novels of Dickens, Flaubert and

Tolstoy, and in the paintings of Courbet and Millet, it began as a progressive force which articulated the rise of the middle class against the vested interests of aristocracy and feudalism in modern industrial society, but it gradually became a conservative force in Europe and North America as the middle class consolidated against a more and more restless and assertive working class for whom realism did not so much reflect the reality of the world as articulate the dominant liberal-capitalist ideology of the bourgeoisie. In reaction to this dominance of bourgeois realism, progressive aesthetic movements took two key directions – one into modernist abstraction and the other into social realism – and both were fuelled by the successive upheavals which marked the first half of the twentieth century, especially after World War One and the Russian Revolution when the class struggles of the 1920s and 1930s witnessed the international spread of socialist ideals and political practice and the reactionary rise of fascism.

Modernism developed around the avant-garde search for deeper, more complex patterns than those of the visible world – with Cubism, for example, searching for abstract forms in the universe of physical objects, Dada parodying the dehumanising tendencies of commodity culture, and Surrealism exploring the unconscious of the human psyche. In Italy, the Futurism of Filippo Tommasi Marinetti and Umberto Boccioni searched for abstract ways of representing the machine-based rhythms and speed of everyday life in the modern metropolis. All such movements were driven by a determination to break with the bourgeois realist aesthetics and thematic concerns of the past, especially through motifs of abstraction and dislocation. In cinema, this determination was evident from Robert Wiene's Weimar German expressionist *The Cabinet of Dr Caligari* (1919) to Sergei Eisenstein's *Battleship Potemkin* (1925) and Salvador Dalí and Luis Buñuel's surrealist *Un chien andalou* (1929). Most forms of modernism tended towards socialist or communist politics and towards a revolutionary internationalist agenda in which modernist artistic experimentation was intended as a vehicle of social and political change on behalf of the working class. In Italy, however, Futurism deviated from this general tendency into a vision of social and political revolution as the rejuvenation of Italy as a great nation, the inauguration of a charismatic dictatorship, and a pledge that 'We will glorify war – the world's only hygiene' (Marinetti 1993: 147) – in sum, support for Mussolini's regime.

Meanwhile, social realism, with which neorealism would be identified after World War Two, continued to believe in the ability of art, literature and film to meaningfully represent the visible world as such and thereby to comment on modern capitalist society, especially urban society, with a view to reforming it. Concerned very much with the present day, it flourished especially during the Great Depression of the 1930s. The hardships and heroic endurance of working-class life were celebrated by the paintings of Mexican muralists such as Diego Rivera and José Clemente Orozco, the photography of Paul Strand and Dorothea Lange, and documentary films such as Alberto Cavalcanti's *Coal Face* (1935) and Pare Lorentz's *The Plow that Broke the Plains* (1936).

Such documentaries were one of the most important creative directions taken in international film culture of the day where the search for cinematic realism was a central preoccupation, and where realism appeared in different forms and with different ideological agendas in British documentary film, Weimar German avant-garde film, the Soviet montage school, French poetic realism and Hollywood gangster films. In most of these manifestations, realism was associated with leftist or progressive causes – as in the association of the Soviet montage school with Russian communism in the 1920s or of the poetic realism of Jean Renoir with the socialist Popular Front of the 1930s. It was therefore frequently presumed to be an inherently critical aesthetic for social change even though the relationship between realism and politics was actually convoluted. The classical Hollywood cinema of the 1920s and 1930s for the most part masked a conservative ideology behind a superficially realist visual style, as did the aesthetics of Weimar German consumer culture, the so-called *Neue Sachlichkeit* (New Objectivity) against which Georg Lukács, Theodor Adorno, Siegfried Kracauer and Walter Benjamin directed their energies as cultural critics until 1933. In this context of a struggle for realism between left and right, fascist regimes in both Germany and Italy learned to appropriate realist aesthetics for their own ends (as in Italy, Mussolini's regime also learned to selectively incorporate and encourage Futurism). As has been shown in recent analyses of Walter Ruttmann's *Berlin, Symphony of a City* (1927), the realist aesthetics of some of the most famous Weimar German films were ideologically ambivalent and were easily co-opted by the Nazis (see Gaughan 2003; Strathausen 2003). In 1933, Ruttmann accepted an invitation from Emilio Cecchi, the director of the Cines studio, to travel to Italy to make *Acciaio* (1933), a semi-documentary about industrial workers living contentedly under fascism, and later he collaborated with Nazi documentarist Leni Riefenstahl on *Triumph of the Will* (1934) and *Olympia* (1938). But this was realism, carefully-controlled and laced with a firmly authoritarian spirit, and it appealed to fascist regimes precisely because it had an aura of cultural and popular authenticity due to its association with movements for social improvement in other societies and in the days before fascism. In Italy too, this regulated cinematic realism was present: in strong form, in LUCE documentaries, and in weaker form in the location filming for feature films of Camerini and Blasetti, as well as in historical epics such as Genina's *The Siege of the Alcazar* (*L'assedio dell'Alcazar*, 1940) which mixed location filming and newsreel footage of the Spanish Civil War. Far from being precursors of neorealism, however, these films were antithetical to it on every level except that of visual form.

The emergence of neorealism

As the outbreak of World War Two approached, the subordination of Italian feature film production to the agendas of the fascist regime reached a peak. Even those directors whose work had most interestingly employed realism, such as Camerini, retreated to increasing visual stylisation and literary adaptations which spurned the realities of life in contemporary Italy. The aestheticism of the so-called 'calligraphist' films of the early 1940s such as Camerini's *A Romantic Adventure*, Renato Castellani's *A Pistol Shot* (*Un colpo di pistola*, 1941), Luigi Chiarini's *Five Moons Street* (*Via delle cinque lune*, 1942), Mario Soldati's *Malombra* (1942), Ferdinando Maria Poggioli's *Yes, Madam* (*Sissignora*, 1942) and Alberto Lattuada's *Giacomo the Idealist* (*Giacomo l'idealista*, 1943), reflected a defensive art-for-art's-sake attitude in Italian cinema as the country was buffeted by the winds of war. This prompted the mainly younger generation of critics and filmmakers gathered under the umbrella of the *Cinema* journal to lament what they saw as an increasingly dull bourgeois complacency. In the early 1940s, the intellectual climate in Italy became increasingly skeptical of the fascist regime and critical opinion on the cinema, as articulated in *Cinema* and the *Bianco e nero*, became increasingly impatient with the cinematic status quo. Overrun by comedies, literary melodramas and historical epics, the cinema was seen to have deserted any interest in the realist representation of Italy and its people. For Mario Alicata and Giuseppe De Santis, both of whom were communists, the time had come for a decisive move to an unambiguously realist cinema, a revolutionary aesthetic which would provide an antidote to bourgeois stasis by staking its commitment to the lives and landscapes of ordinary working-class and peasant Italians. The essay in which they made their call for this new cinema, 'Truth and Poetry: Verga and Italian Cinema', was published in *Cinema* on 10 October 1941. Alicata and De Santis voiced their frustration with the 'silly pretensions' of 'pure' filmmakers, especially those such as Camerini and Soldati who had proven themselves capable of interesting realist innovations in the past. The best cinema, they asserted, retains a link with real people and places through a faithfulness to great literature, specifically the classics of nineteenth-century European naturalism in the novel and on stage – Flaubert, Chekhov, Dickens, Ibsen and, most importantly of all, the Italian writer Giovanni Verga (1840–1922). Verga, a Sicilian born to a wealthy, landed family in Catania, attained the status of founding father of Italian *verismo* through his short story collections such as *Vita dei campi* (1880) and *Novelle rusticane* (1883), and his novel *I Malavoglia* (1881), in which his subject was the detailed representation of the local character of Sicilian society and landscape, especially as experienced by Sicily's distinctly poor and marginalised peasantry. Verga's literature had been central to *verismo*'s rejection of the classical Italian literature of Gabriele D'Annunzio and, for Alicata and De Santis, could also offer Italian filmmakers an escape from the 'moribund bourgeois state' of current cinema, especially the clichéd urban milieu of its socially pretentious comedies. In cinema, realism in this mode could be found both in America, in the Depression-era social portraits of King Vidor's *The Crowd* (1928) and *Our Daily Bread* (1934), and in France, in the recent films of Renoir and Carné, whom Alicata and De Santis singled out for admiration.

Of course, Alicata and De Santis' call for a new realism did not immediately produce a neorealist cinema. Their version of cinematic realism gave a priority to the well-crafted narrative which did not find a perfect reflection in the neorealist films of the immediate post-war period which were, for the most part, non-literary in inspiration and which eschewed careful scripting. Rossellini's *Rome, Open City*, *Paisà* and *Germany Year Zero* and De Sica's *Shoeshine*, *Bicycle Thieves* and *Umberto D* fuelled the dominant critical consensus of the post-war period which stressed the primarily visual character of neorealism, a realism not only not disposed to traditional narrative but even antithetical to it, as André Bazin and Cesare Zavattini constantly asserted. In its devotion to Verga, the realism proposed by Alicata and De Santis was also, by implication, primarily rural in its preoccupation – indeed, Alicata and De Santis specifically criticise the decadent *urban* milieu of comedies by Camerini and others and their clichéd images of the ubiquitous fashionable nightclubs of Rome's Via Nazionale. On the other hand, the literary new realism required by Alicata and De Santis did find a clear manifestation in Luchino Visconti's screen adaptations of James

M. Cain's *The Postman Always Rings Twice* for *Ossessione* (co-scripted by Visconti with Alicata and others) and Verga's *I Malavoglia* for *La terra trema*.

Signs of an impending cinematic rebirth in Italy became increasingly clear in the final year of the fascist government in Rome before its collapse in July 1943. Each of the three most important directors to be associated with neorealism after the war – Rossellini, De Sica and Visconti – directed a feature film between the summers of 1942 and 1943. As we will see below, Rossellini's *Man of the Cross* (*L'uomo dalla croce*, 1943) displayed certain formal characteristics which seemed to anticipate the neorealism which would fully emerge with the Liberation, while De Sica's *The Children Are Watching Us* (*I bambini ci guardano*, 1944) anticipated both neorealism's formal approach and its thematic questioning of the established social order. The most famous of the three, Luchino Visconti's *Ossessione*, was arguably neorealist even before the Liberation. As the end of the fascist regime approached, the fragile ideological consistency of Italian cinema which it had managed to engineer began to collapse. Even Blasetti anticipated the changing artistic and political climate in directing his melodrama *Four Steps in the Clouds* (*Quattro passi fra le nuvole*, 1942), partly scripted by Zavattini, whose compassionate story of a traveling salesman who befriends a young pregnant girl in working-class Rome left behind the rhetoric of his earlier films in favour of something approaching the modest human realism demanded by *Cinema*. Blasetti's film typified the artistic and political evolution through which some of Italy's established filmmakers would proceed as the fascist regime came to an end.

The emergence of Roberto Rossellini

The early films of Roberto Rossellini (1906–1977) demonstrate a similar evolution by a director at the beginning of his career. The son of a wealthy Roman family, he had begun in cinema as a sound technician, editor and assistant director, before managing, through his acquaintances with Vittorio Mussolini and the producer Franco Riganti, to secure a role co-scripting Alessandrini's celebration of Italian military heroism, *Luciano Serra pilota*. His first significant foray as a director was the documentary *The White Ship* (*La nave bianca*, 1942), made on commission for the Italian navy as a study of conditions on board a hospital ship under fire at sea. The film was made under the supervision of the documentarist Francesco De Robertis, who was in charge of the Navy's Centro Cinematografico in the Ministerio della Marina, and who had himself directed *Uomini sul fondo* (1941), a dramatisation of an underwater rescue from a wrecked submarine which filmed real sailors on location at sea to achieve an effect of understated heroism. Rossellini's *The White Ship*, like De Robertis' film, presented war not so much as a matter of heroic action but in terms of the passive endurance of hardship in the hostile and confined machine-like environment of the ship. The propagandistic potential it might have held in the hands of a more conventional director was, therefore, relatively muted and Rossellini, in later life, always maintained that there was a direct line between its realism and that of his later work, at least on the level of form. Nevertheless, *The White Ship* was a film made on behalf of the fascist regime. If Roy Armes is correct to propose that it was 'designed simply to reassure' where *Rome, Open City* and later Rossellini films were 'designed to probe and attack' (1971: 44), its reassurance was at best indecisive.

Whether Rossellini's *Man of the Cross* was designed to reassure or to probe and attack is not entirely clear. Its somewhat bleak drama centres on a Catholic chaplain serving with Italian tank troops in Russia in the summer of 1942. Here Rossellini moves towards increasing naturalism in portraying the close relationship which inevitably obtains between human being and landscape in a war zone whether for Italian troops lounging on the grass in the summer sun under cover of a grove of trees or for Russian refugees huddled in the stone and timber remnants of a smashed cottage in the midst of a firefight. The film recreates wartime Russia using real footage and intense combat sequences which mimic the documentary authenticity of newsreel both in their images and in their use of richly textured sound to suggest the cacophony of war. There is clearly a relationship between them and Rossellini's representations of the ravages of war on people and places in *Paisà* and *Germany Year Zero* and it is tempting to read Rossellini's realist representation of war as a critique of war, the fulcrum of which is an army chaplain who, while technically an Italian soldier is not at all a soldier in spirit, but an outside observer of suffering. However, the film's realism is not clearly critical. It lacks the authenticity of Rossellini's later films in so far as its location sequences were filmed not in Russia but just outside Rome and its interiors were filmed at Cinecittà using professional actors. It characterises Italian forces serving on the Eastern Front as competent, brave and collegial, and their chaplain, who ministers to wounded soldiers and refugees despite the dangers of battle around him, as an especially selfless man whose religious faith imbues him with calm self-assurance and a capacity for endurance. These characteristics stand him in good

stead to keep his head during battle, but they also equip him to with-
stand the contempt of, and then to forgive, the treacherous Bolsheviks he
encounters whom Rossellini portrays as blind slaves of ideology who have
little real concern for ordinary Russian people. Indeed, Rossellini suggests
that ordinary Russian peasants welcome the Italian army as liberators from
communism and the film's central anti-communist theme is confirmed in
its closing dedication to the military chaplains who have given their lives in
the 'crusade' against the 'godless' Soviet Union.

Thus, *Man of the Cross* is an imperfectly crafted film which fails to speak
with one voice. On the one hand, it begins to reach toward a potentially critical realism; on the other, it is vulgar propaganda which articulates the fundamental anti-communism of the fascist regime and of the Catholic Church.
This ambivalence should perhaps not surprise us for the film was a product
of the final year of Italy's fascist regime in which the regime still held power
but with decreasing effectiveness. Shot between July and September 1942,
and released in June 1943, by which time the Allies had taken North Africa
and were about to invade Sicily, its recognition of the heroism of Italy's
armies must have rung very hollow indeed, as Peter Bondanella has wryly
observed (1993: 35). Rossellini, like other filmmakers of his generation
living under fascism, was forced to negotiate between his desire to make
films at a time when no film could be made that was critical of fascism and
his reluctance to endorse fascism because its politics were not his and
never had been. However, this argument only works if we ignore the film
Rossellini made between *The White Ship* and *Man of the Cross* – that is, *Un
pilota ritorna* (1942) – about which Rossellini never liked to speak after the
war. Within the format of a conventional star vehicle with superficial documentary trappings, that film unambiguously paid tribute to the heroism of
the Italian air force, represented in the dashing figure of Massimo Girotti,
playing a pilot who escapes from a Greek prisoner of war camp. *Un pilota
ritorna* suggests that the formal and thematic characteristics of Rossellini's
wartime films cannot be explained simply in terms of increasing realist
experimentation nor only in terms of Rossellini's conscious negotiation
of life under fascism: it must also be explained in terms of errors of political and personal judgment made by Rossellini during the war. Rossellini
was not a very young man when he came to direct his first films and must
have realised the implications of working within the genre of the war film
during a time of war, of all genres he could have worked in. He must also
have been aware of the implications of being closely associated with such
figures as Vittorio Mussolini, who partly scripted *Un pilota ritorna*, and De

Robertis, who took charge of film production for Mussolini when the fascist regime was forced to relocate from Rome to Venice to escape the advancing Allies in the autumn of 1943. In subsequent years, Rossellini himself tended to downplay his activities during the war, explaining that in making films then he had always tried to remain beyond the grip of fascist control. In a climate where fascism demanded unambivalent commitment but where such commitment was unthinkable, crafted ambiguity was the only possible refuge. Rossellini worked within the system, but only just.

The emergence of Vittorio De Sica

Vittorio De Sica (1901–1974) arrived at feature-film directing from a different direction to that of Rossellini. In the 1920s he had begun as a leading actor with the successful satirical theatre company ZaBum before making the transition to the screen with his first major film role in Camerini's *What Rascals Men Are!*. His good looks and air of upper-middle-class refinement contributed to the success of Camerini's sentimental comedies and it was this genre which De Sica modified on behalf of the emerging generation of filmmakers who would mature in the post-war period. After four uneventful directorial debuts – including *Red Roses* (*Rose scarlatte*, 1940), a theatrical comedy adapted for the screen and co-directed with Giuseppe Amato, and *Teresa Venerdi* (1941), a conventional sentimental social comedy to which the screenwriter Cesare Zavattini made an uncredited script contribution – De Sica directed *The Children Are Watching Us*, filmed in the spring of 1943 but not released until the following year. De Sica and Zavattini had first met in Verona in 1935 while working on Camerini's *I'll Give a Million*, but *The Children Are Watching Us* inaugurated their close working partnership as director and writer. An innovative film which introduced a new thematic instability and questioning into the cinema as the fascist era came to an end, it concerns the break-up of the family of a young boy, Prico, due to his mother's marital infidelity and his father's suicide, both of which leave him to fend for himself, facing an uncertain future in a harsh adult world. The film inherited the social milieu of 1930s sentimental comedies, focusing not on the urban-industrial working class or impoverished rural peasants who would become the standard characters of neorealist cinema but on a middle-class family who are materially well-off enough to employ a maid. Though much of the film takes place in interiors, the suburbs of Rome where they live consist of respectable apartment blocks and pleasant parks where mothers and children walk and play in the sun. Their weekend getaway is the beach resort of Alassio where the urban bourgeoisie pass their leisure time at restaurants, performances and dances. Adulthood and childhood alike are suggested as potentially idyllic, just as they were by Camerini.

However, De Sica does not allow this sense to linger for long. Instead he undermines it with an innovatively frank representation of the dysfunctional Italian family and the irresolvable strains of modern life in Rome which immediately place the film beyond the ideological confines of most cinema of the fascist era and endow it with a measure of critical power lacking in the films of Camerini and beyond the ambiguity of Rossellini's *Man of the Cross*. This critical power, of course, is not directly antagonistic to the fascist regime – indeed, De Sica was liked by the fascist minister with responsibility for film, Pavolini, and was his first choice to run the regime's film industry in Venice in 1943 before the job was given to Francesco De Robertis. But this was before the release of *The Children Are Watching Us* which firmly transformed De Sica from poster boy to critically intelligent filmmaker. Although the film made no mention of government, politics or war, and confined itself entirely to domestic melodrama, it ran counter to the fascist projection of the happy nuclear family as backbone of Italian society and of the modern Italian state as a community of productive citizens. Its images of dysfunctionality were all the more cutting in that the majority of the action was presented from the point of view of the young boy not only narratologically but through cinematography, replicating his visual perspective as a diminutive child in a physically domineering environment. The film initially attributes more responsibility for his misfortune to his fickle and unfaithful mother than it does to his dutiful and loving father – her infidelity is presented as the root cause of their troubles and many scenes emphasise the intense bond of paternal love which links father and son in her absence – but by the end of the film, as Prico's father commits suicide out of shame at the break-up of his marriage, the film is equally negative in its representation of women and men. Its ending is remarkably discomforting: Prico's mother arrives to reclaim her son from the orphanage in whose care the boy's father has left him; but in the final shot, Prico refuses to forgive his weeping mother, walking away on his own in a manner which suggests a mature resolve and forced independence out of keeping with his small size. The priests who have been looking after him look on benevolently: there is no heavy-handed recuperation of the narrative into a political or religious agenda as in Rossellini's *Man of the Cross*. Instead, De Sica clearly anticipates neorealism in his interest in the ability of social dysfunction and moral crisis to resist neat resolution. *The Children Are Watching Us* stands as the most artistically sophisticated and ideologically progressive film of the fascist era after Visconti's *Ossessione*. In the final year of the fascist regime, with the war firmly turned against the Axis powers, it began to suggest that all was not well in the state of Italy in ways which earlier films had not been able to.

2   NEOREALISM'S FIRST PHASE

Ossessione

The destabilisation of positive cinematic images of fascist Italy intensified with Luchino Visconti's *Ossessione*, which began filming on 15 June
1942. Visconti (1906–1976) came from an aristocratic background, the
son of the Duke of Modrone, and spent his young adulthood as a man of
leisure traveling extensively in Europe. Visiting Paris regularly from 1932,
he became acquainted with the city's artistic and intellectual social circles
and through a friendship with the designer Coco Chanel was introduced to
the director Jean Renoir, gaining his first professional experience in cinema
as assistant director on Renoir's *Une partie de campagne*. The extended
periods he spent in France familiarised him with the avant-garde work of
Buñuel, Cocteau, Man Ray, Pudovkin and Eisenstein and he developed
Marxist and communist political convictions in sympathy with the leftist
Popular Front of the day, especially after the outbreak of the Spanish Civil
War (1936–39). As Roy Armes has put it, Visconti's own directorial career,
beginning with *Ossessione*, displayed 'a life-time's concern with the poor
and underprivileged' (1971: 119), a concern no doubt partly inspired by
Visconti's recognition of his own marginalised position in Italian fascist
society as a homosexual. By the early 1940s, Visconti was very much in
tune with the call for a new cinematic realism made by Alicata and De
Santis in *Cinema*. Writing in the journal himself, he was critical of white
telephone and calligraphist films and praised the French poetic realism of
Renoir, Carné and Clair. Indeed, it was thanks to Renoir that the immediate inspiration for *Ossessione* arose – the French director gave Visconti
a French translation of James M. Cain's novel *The Postman Always Rings*

Twice which was then adapted for the screen by Visconti in collaboration with Alicata, De Santis, Antonio Pietrangeli and Gianni Puccini, all of whom shared strong leftist and anti-fascist convictions, and who set out to redirect its American subject into a critique of Italian fascist society.

This process involved a number of transformations of the novel. Cain's three key characters – Frank, Cora and Nick – became *Ossessione*'s Gino, Giovanna and Bragana, and the action was transposed from Southern California to Italy's Po valley. The novel's narrative was reorganised to focus more on the obsessive romance of Gino and Giovanna than on the police investigation of their murder of her husband Bragana – a modification which, in playing down the official authority of the state, carried clear implications in a film produced during a moment of crisis for the fascist regime. Finally, the novel's first-person narrator was removed and its already sparse dialogue minimised to foreground the documentation of physical and social surroundings which were important elements in Cain's book. These changes allowed Visconti to concentrate on the visual representation of landscape, especially through an innovative use of long-takes, deep-focus cinematography, and fluid and sweeping camera movements.

Often this visual style was used to suggest a fatalistic relationship between the film's protagonists and their surroundings. *Ossessione* avoids conventional beauty and grandeur in its representation of the Po valley, presenting instead a haunting and windswept terrain whose unromanticised bleakness reinforces the sense of doom which pervades the narrative from the outset. Visconti works against those images of comfort and productivity, social harmony and moral goodness, which dominated fascist-era cinema. Certain images of a harmonious and contented Italy do appear – for example, at the singing contest in Ancona where Bragana wins first prize, and at the busy trattoria soon after Bragana's death where families eat and children play in the sun. But these are undercut by the planning, commission and cover-up of murder which they mask and which pollute every image of normality in the film with more than a hint of corruption. Meanwhile, the film's focus on the humble lives of rural peasants contrasts with the wealth and luxury of white telephone and calligraphist films. The relationship of Gino and Giovanna arises in part out of a shared experience of poverty: he has been a casual laborer but spends most of his time as an unemployed drifter, the antithesis of the fascist ideal of the dutiful worker; she married Bragana only because she was penniless and implies that she used to have to beg men for food in return for sex. Meanwhile, their mutual lust and their eventual murder of Bragana are an affront to Catholic morality and challenge the myth of the happy nuclear family even more boldly than De Sica's *The Children Are Watching Us*.

Their sexual intensity is a function of their restless desperation, which Visconti evokes through oppositions of indoor and outdoor space, domesticity and mobility. On one level, these are articulated through strong visual contrasts between the low chiaroscuro lighting and cluttered rooms of the trattoria's interior and the bright sunlight and natural vistas of the Po valley outside. But the oppositions also work at a deeper narratological level. The trattoria is an oppressive environment for Giovanna, but one in which she ultimately wants to stay; the outside world of romantic hobo wandering is a liberating one for Gino but one which he is ultimately drawn to give up. Over the course of the film, Gino's mobility encourages her dissatisfaction and her plan to kill her husband while Giovanna's domesticity entices him to stay in one place and do the killing for her. Just as in Cain's novel, this pattern of oppositions draws upon a tension between the traditionalism of the trattoria and its rural setting, on the one hand, and urban modernity, on the other. In the opening sequence, the truck rolling along a lonely highway is accompanied by discordant strings and drums which suggest a menacing and foreboding invasion of the pre-modern emptiness of the Po valley. Its arrival brings a further invasion of the domestic routine of the trattoria by another stranger, Gino, who is filmed by a striking crane shot and then a smoothly-constructed series of tracking shots as he approaches and enters the building, hears the singing Giovanna in the kitchen, and stalks in like a hunter in search of prey.

The sequence emphasises the isolated situation of the trattoria, sitting on a trunk road, upon which it depends for business, somewhere near the city of Ferrara. This isolation places the film's main action outside of the urban centres of fascist authority, providing a place apart from the mainstream of society in which Gino and Giovanna can almost hope to get away with murder. But throughout the film there is a sense that the law will inevitably catch up with them not only because the police are on their trail but because the isolated and traditional rural environment in which the trattoria is situated is under threat from inexorable forces. Indeed, although *Ossessione* is often admired for its images of rural Italy, it actually spends a considerable amount of time in urban settings – not only the commercial centre of Ferrara but also the bustling industrial port of Ancona – and the trattoria is not so much a sign of the pure countryside as it is a point of transit in what appears to be an obsolescent rural environment. Bicycles, the locals' preferred mode of transport, are under threat from heavy traffic and billboards for Fiat and Pirelli line roadside fields. These and the actual trucks and cars which criss-cross the countryside point to the increasing mobility of the Italian people and the expansion of transport which characterised the fascist era. The construction of the nation's first autostrada in 1923, the launch of the first people's car, the Fiat Topolino, in 1936, and the regime's encouragement of train travel as a means of tourism for the nation's crowded city residents facilitated travel within and between cities and identified fascism with modernisation. But they also had the effect of increasing the city's penetration of daily rural life. In *Ossessione*, the flat and quiet expanses of the Po valley seem resistant to this modernising process and to fascism. Indeed, Visconti's representation anticipates the real historical role of the Po valley during the liberation of Italy as one of the most important sites of anti-fascist resistance and, of course, its moving description in the final sequence of Rossellini's *Paisà* as a natural wilderness riven by the negative 'modernising' influence of war.

In *Ossessione*, the disruptive influence of the urban on the rural is not so dramatic but it is evident. The film's motif of increasing mechanical mobility suggests the threat, but it is also implied in the progressive complication of Gino's efforts to wander. These begin when he leaves Giovanna and the trattoria to resume his hobo life. He meets the 'Spaniard' on the train to Ancona, striking up a refreshingly carefree friendship, formed 'on the road' and based upon their shared belief in spontaneous wandering, non-conformism and the rejection of material wealth and comfort. That rejection is directly linked to the politics of the left: as co-scriptwriter Mario Alicata explained, the Spaniard's name and his reference to having 'worked in Spain a long time' were intended to imply that he had fought against fascism in the Spanish Civil War while his purchase of a train ticket for the penniless Gino was intended as a socialist gesture of workers' solidarity. That solidarity also had homosexual overtones: not only do Gino and the Spaniard share values and an emotional bond almost as intense as that between Gino and Giovanna but, in Ancona, they share a double bed and Gino's body is presented as the subject of the Spaniard's erotic appreciation. The film therefore presents Gino with two entirely opposed sets of spatial and ideological coordinates: Giovanna, domesticity and the respectable private enterprise of the trattoria; the Spaniard, mobility and the rejection of the social and moral status quo. In Ancona the latter option seems the more attractive and the city initially appears as the starting point of a new adventure, a busy port whose mixture of tightly-packed buildings, ships, factories, streetcars and pedestrians give it a physical and

Fig. 1 Gino and the Spaniard see the port city of Ancona in *Ossessione*

social density and a sense of opportunity which contrasts with the rural space of the Po valley. But this density soon turns out to be an entrapping one when Gino, in one of the urban chance encounters of which neorealist cinema was so fond, accidentally bumps into Giovanna and Bragana while working as a sandwich man. The liberating possibilities of Ancona and of life with the Spaniard are cut short and Gino is drawn back into murderous intrigue.

During the singing contest which shortly follows, it becomes clear that the reunification of Gino and Giovanna poses a terminal danger to her husband. Visconti uses depth-of-field and subtle camera movement to counterpoint their deadly conspiracy in the foreground of his shots with the jovial singing, laughing and drinking of Bragana and the crowds in the background. By the time a champagne toast is made to Bragana's victory, his death is a *fait accompli*. We see the three set off for home together, the drunk and singing Bragana driving for a while, then getting sick, before Gino takes the wheel. But Visconti does not bother to show us the actual killing – he cuts straight to the following morning as Gino and Giovanna explain to the police that the drunken Bragana lost control of his car and only luck prevented them too from losing their lives. With their return to the trattoria, Giovanna is fulfilled but Gino has traveled in an empty circle. The murder has not resolved their dissatisfaction. Her domestic instincts and his inclination to roam are as antithetical as ever. While old men gossip and play bowls in the sunlight outside, they argue in long interior scenes in which the shuttered windows of the trattoria create a night-like chiaroscuro inside. The camera continuously tracks and pans their bodies, pacing to and fro before alternating close-ups reveal their contradictory positions – Giovanna pleading, 'Be reasonable. Business must go on!', but Gino retorting, 'It's no job to be the keeper of a dead man's house!' Twice more, Gino turns down chances to get out. In the first, the local priest, Father Remigio suggests that, for the sake of social appearances and moral propriety, he and Giovanna should separate for some time before announcing their engagement; but this suggestion only makes the Catholic Church seem incompetent and hypocritical as it does not occur to Remigio for a moment that he is aiding and abetting two killers. In the second, the Spaniard makes a final effort to persuade Gino to join him on the road, proposing that they can find casual work near Genoa working on a new highway which is being constructed, but his plan is scuppered when Gino punches him on the mouth and he is forced to walk away towards the horizon in disgust.

Appropriately enough, the final complication of Gino and Giovanna's relationship comes in another city – Ferrara – where Gino strikes up another liaison by buying an ice cream for an attractive young woman, Anita, in a city-centre park. Unlike Ancona, an informal and energetic port, Ferrara, the largest city in the Po region, appears as a commercial and administrative centre. It is the home of police headquarters, and its centre is dominated by the Palazzo Schifanoia, renaissance palace of the local aristocratic Este family, which sits prominently in the background of many shots as Gino waits for Giovanna to emerge from the Milan Insurance Company. When Giovanna offers to share the money from her husband's life insurance policy, Gino suspects her of using him. Though he has rejected the socialist alternative offered by the Spaniard, he also rejects her offer of capital and opts instead for a new direction, storming off in anger to the home of Anita in the nearby working-class neighborhood of the via Saraceni. Here he encounters a final chance to get out.

On her dresser, Anita keeps a photo of a sailor who may be her husband, but she works as a prostitute and assumes that Gino is just another client until, talking at length, it seems that they have a common bond. Their quickly-established intimacy leads him to confess the murder to her and another 'new beginning' for Gino seems on the cards. But this, all too predictably, is also ruptured when Gino is confronted in the street outside by a furious Giovanna who threatens to report him to the police for having betrayed her with another woman. Visconti uses a series of extreme close-ups to underline the emotional intensity of the action and an abrupt cut to an aerial shot when Gino slaps Giovanna in anger, which reveals them surrounded by a crowd converging on their now public dispute. The busy streets of Ferrara become a backdrop for their mutual shame and its haphazard rooftops the route of Gino's escape from the detectives who arrive on the scene. The existential intensity and crowded situations of the city add to the gathering desperation. But this intensity is perhaps most acutely felt with regard to Anita, deserted by Gino but selfless enough to save him from the police by lying that he was a client who didn't pay. Her public admission of prostitution, in order to save a man she barely knows, is a moment of dignified pathos, reinforced by her bowed head and a soundtrack of gentle strings, which makes Gino's rejection of her a sign of cowardice and reckless self-indulgence.

Back at the trattoria, for one last time, the sense of narratological circularity and frustration which has been building since the opening scene now comes to a head as Giovanna's announcement that she is pregnant seems to offer her and Gino a solid base for their relationship and an opportunity for moral rejuvenation: 'You see we stole one life but we're going to give one back!' Emerging from a night of reflection spent in the riverbed outside the trattoria, Gino seems resolved to finally settle down and the gently panning camera, following their stroll across flat, featureless expanses of sand, in the soft morning light, seems to offer the Po valley, finally, as a scene of resolution and calm which offers positive relief from the anger of the city. A series of driving shots, which recall those of the truck in the opening sequence, show them fleeing the trattoria, resolved to escape the police and make a new life with their child. But this image of mobility, which seems one of hope, is soon turned to one of despair: stuck behind a large truck, inhaling its fumes, Gino makes a move to beat the traffic by overtaking it but crashes off the side of the road, killing Giovanna in a cruel reversal of their earlier murder of her husband. Just as the police arrive to arrest him, he lays her dead and bloodied body on the road, now swept by two waves of destruction and grief which have scarred the Po valley landscape irrevocably.

This sequence of events closes with harsh finality a narrative constituted entirely of defeats. During the film's limited public release in May

Fig. 2 Gino and Giovanna in the riverbed in *Ossessione*

1943, with the course of the war clearly turning in favour of the Allies and with Mussolini's days apparently numbered, Guido Aristarco's review of the film in the *Corriere Padano* newspaper praised *Ossessione*'s 'intimate fusion of style and human values' and its rejection of the superficiality and light entertainment of fascist-era cinema. Not surprisingly, however, the film was received with deep displeasure by fascists and the Catholic Church. The production and its members had been watched by police because of their known anti-fascist associations – indeed, in December 1942, just after principal shooting, Alicata and Puccini were arrested and imprisoned in the Regina Coeli jail in Rome for eight months. The initial script of the film which the authorities had approved had contained key scenes which might have allayed controversy, showing Gino and Giovanna marrying at the last minute before her death and Gino then being convicted of murder, but there was no sign of these in the final version of the film. Vittorio Mussolini famously stormed out of its Rome premiere declaring, 'This is not Italy!', and screenings were blocked by a number of local fascist and Catholic authorities before the film was withdrawn from distribution entirely until after the war (see Servadio 1980: 81). The original negative was removed by the authorities to the new Republic of Salò and only Visconti's own duplicate guaranteed the film's survival.

Although some historians have been reluctant to describe *Ossessione* as truly neorealist, preferring to reserve the term for films made in the immediate aftermath of the war, its suppression, in combination with its formal and thematic innovation, should give *Ossessione* at least as much claim to neorealist status as *Rome, Open City* or later films. Indeed, it was one thing to produce an anti-fascist film after the war, quite another while the fascists were still in power. Certain aspects of the film – its use of extreme close-ups for emotional impact or its bleakly fatalistic narrative structure – do not fit neatly with models of neorealism which emphasise its neutral camera style or its loose and chance-based stories. But anomalous characteristics are evident in every neorealist film and do not cancel out the innovative combination of strategies in *Ossessione* which later neorealist films would expand upon – location filming, working-class subjects, the study of alienation, critical perspectives on Italian society informed by leftist politics, and a lack of moral judgement of characters and situations.

Although *Ossessione* began filming in mid-1942 when Allied victory in the war was far from certain, its dystopian images of Italian society anticipated the impending collapse of fascism and the social and political crisis which would ensue in the immediate post-war years. The film's release in May 1943 came just two months before the Allied invasion of Sicily on 9 July, the fall of Mussolini's government in Rome, and his arrest on 25 July. Although the country still faced nearly two years of brutal occupation and warfare, Italy's military defeat was already clear both in Russia and North Africa; the day-to-day operation of the fascist regime was crumbling; the economy was ruined by inflation and spreading industrial unrest in the cities; and severe food rationing was already depriving Italians of basic nutritional needs. *Ossessione* therefore emerged into a highly volatile situation which already resembled in many of its key features that which would prevail in 1945 when Rossellini and others made the first neorealist films of the post-war era. In this context, it did not matter that the film kept its socialist politics veiled. It was more important to portray a social and political moment in Italian history grinding to a halt. In the film's final seconds, Gino is arrested, but our final image of his anguish has a dangerous instability and the authority of the state seems far from secure. His struggle comes to an end but we suspect that another is just beginning.

Rome, Open City

After the premiere of *Ossessione*, events moved quickly towards the collapse of Italian fascism. On 25 July 1943 Mussolini was arrested and his government replaced by a new regime appointed by King Vittorio Emmanuele III. In September, with Italy declaring a formal armistice with the Allies, the German army rescued Mussolini from his Italian captors, occupied Rome, and re-established a much-reduced Italian fascist regime, the Republic of Salò, near Venice. Nine months of bitter warfare ensued before the liberation of Rome in June 1944 and nine more before the liberation of all of Italy in the spring of 1945. While the Allies pushed slowly northwards from Sicily, tens of thousands of anti-fascist partisans initiated their own guerilla resistance to the Germans. These anti-fascists came from a diverse range of political backgrounds: the Communist Party was dominant, but Socialists, Christian Democrats and members of the radical social-democratic Action Party also played important roles. These groups worked together to defeat a common enemy but each had its own view of how Italian society should move forward once peace was secured.

Some neorealists did become involved in the resistance – Visconti, for example, was arrested in 1944 and only narrowly escaped a death sentence – but most of the leading directors did not and none saw real combat. As the country emerged from fascism, however, filmmakers, like all Italians, had to adjust to the material, social, political and artistic realities of liberation. Although Italy did not suffer as much physical devastation as did Germany, the war had caused substantial loss of life – most estimates place Italy's total death toll at around 300,000 – and considerable damage to many of its cities and towns (see Messenger 1989). Allied aerial bombing, for example, destroyed 25,000 homes in Turin in 1942 alone and displaced 500,000 inhabitants from Milan (Clark 1996: 289). Liberation brought a widespread sense of trauma and relief, elation and guilt, among the people and, for a time at least, a profound sense of opportunity for Italy to start afresh. Cinema shared in this sense of opportunity. For Elio Vittorini, it could now answer the 'hunger for reality' which had built up through 22 years of fascism by engaging with post-war Italian society with a renewed sense of social and ethical responsibility and without fear of the censors (see Micchichè 1975: 303). This understanding of cinema informed the foundation of the tellingly-titled new magazine *Film d'oggi* (*Film Today*) in June 1945, a publication whose mostly Communist associates included De Santis, Lizzani, Puccini, Antonioni and De Sica. Post-war cinema would seek to overcome the stylisation, heroic rhetoric and literary tedium which had dominated cinema of the fascist era. Naturally, because it relied on personnel who had trained and worked before the war, neorealism would not entail a complete rejection of all that had gone before, but cinema did now exist in a new political and cultural context in which filmmakers were able to reclaim realism from its fascist appropriation in order to re-direct it to the urgent social conditions of the day. The moment was therefore one of 'rupture and renaissance', as Bazin has described it (1971a: 19), in which there was both a political break and a rejuvenation of realist film form.

In the first instance, as John J. Michalczyk has explained, 'the purpose of the neorealist in filmmaking was *to witness* the ills of society and then *to state* them before the public in order to raise their consciousness (1986: 14). This broad strategy would easily contain a number of approaches – Visconti's interest in the transgression of social and moral norms and his mixing of issues of class antagonism and human fate; Rossellini's strongly moral and spiritual neorealism, reliant on subjective characterisation; and De Sica's warmly sentimental neorealism, given to an inter-personal ethics of tolerance and understanding rather than a political programme. For Visconti and other neorealists such as De Santis and Lizzani, the immediate post-war moment represented a historic opportunity to radically transform Italy into a new socialist society; for others, especially De Sica and Rossellini, that moment provided a decisive new context in which to make a moral cinema and engage with reality in a time of crisis.

Like many of his peers, Rossellini experienced the fall of fascism and the liberation as a period of personal, as well as national, transformation. After the war he usually dated the start of his directorial career to *Rome, Open City*, sometimes acknowledging his earlier films such as *The White Ship* and *Man of the Cross*, but always remaining uncomfortable with *Un pilota ritorna*. In late 1943 and 1944 he became associated with the *Cinema* group and came to enthusiastically embrace the emerging post-war reorientation of realism. This was a time of personal penury as the film industry in Rome ground more or less to a halt under the German occupation and Rossellini was effectively out of work, but it was also a time of creative excitement. The opportunity to make the film which would become *Rome, Open City* emerged in the autumn of 1944 through informal discussions between Rossellini and co-scriptwriters Sergio Amidei and Alberto Consiglio, who determined to draw upon recent real-life events to provide an account of the resistance of ordinary Italians to German oppression.

Though principal shooting took place from January 1945, certain footage used in the film – for example, the marching German troops at night in the opening sequence – had actually been filmed by Rossellini in the spring of 1944 while Rome was still occupied. Made on a limited budget, *Rome, Open City* was filmed mostly on location with a mixture of film stock bought on the black market. A shortage of money for film processing prevented Rossellini from viewing rushes during shooting and necessitated a disciplined approach – for example, placing limits on the length and number of takes of each scene. Less than optimal audio recording conditions and equipment gave a flat, raw character to the soundtrack. The variable quality of black market film stock and of film processing led to inconsistencies in the final print, especially in scenes with low light such as those of Manfredi's torture by the Gestapo (see Gallagher 1998: 136, 140). But these 'shortcomings' conspired to produce a finished film with a striking sense of immediacy and frugality which only enhanced its meaning.

Meanwhile, the narrative was based closely on actual events during the occupation, especially the real-life execution of the resistant priest Don Giuseppe Morosini, in April 1944, and the shooting of a pregnant woman by German troops on Rome's Viale Giulio Cesare. Many of the film's locations were chosen because they might plausibly have been frequented by those real-life figures – for example, the church of Don Pietro (Aldo Fabrizi) on the Via Casilina, and the nearby street on which Pina (Anna Magnani) is shot by German soldiers, both in the working-class Prenestina district southeast of Rome's historic centre. Other locations were 'borrowed' for filming as, for example, in the case of the apartment near the Piazza di Spagna, in which the Germans search for Manfredi, which was the real-life apartment of Sergio Amidei. Finally, Rossellini cast his professional leads against type for deliberate realist effect. Anna Magnani and Aldo Fabrizi were well-known comic stars of the light-hearted *la rivista* theatre, but in *Rome, Open City* their stardom is demystified and rewritten in the direction of tragedy and senseless death. And, in any case, Rossellini made a policy of only allowing his actors to see their lines at the last minute and shooting in short sequences with little preparation and very few takes (see Rossellini's interview from 1954 in Hllier 1985: 209–12).

Much of the film's meaning, however, derived from the strategic contrast of this multi-faceted realism with more traditional elements. The influence of *la rivista* is also evident in the film's narrative structure, especially its typological characterisation of good and evil characters. The Italian people are lovable and earthy types, given to moments of comic distraction, as when Don Pietro knocks out a sick old man with a pan in order to conceal guns from the Germans in his bed. Rossellini's Germans are uniformly demonised and his Romans righteously united against them – only a few barely-delineated Italian fascists complicate the picture, and Marina, the young Italian who fraternises with the enemy, is portrayed as a pitiable victim of Ingrid's Nazi treachery. In contrast to Italian authenticity, Rossellini emphasises Nazi classical decadence and warped self-absorption. Surrounded by cognac, cigarettes and candlelight, German officers drink themselves into morose stupors in their luxury lounge. Consumed with self-hate, one rants, 'We can do nothing but kill. We have sown Europe with corpses and hatred blossoms from the graves. Everywhere there's hatred. We're devoured by hatred, without hope. We shall all perish without hope.' In a strategy perhaps aided by the fact that Rossellini's cinematographer, Ubaldo Arata, had also filmed Camerini's *L'ultima avventura* (1932) and Alessandrini's *Luciano Serra pilota*, many scenes associate the villainy of the Nazis with ornate indoor space and a rich *mise-en-scène* reminiscent of white telephone films of the 1930s. Indeed, scenes set in Gestapo headquarters on the via Tasso were reconstructed in a makeshift film studio in a basement on the via degli Avignonesi and contribute to an opposition between, on the one hand, rich indoor *mise-en-scène* as a sign of the enemy's cowardice and inhumanity and, on the other, outdoor space as a site of Italian resistance and goodness. This opposition becomes clear after Pina's heroic death when the film's tone shifts markedly into righteous indignation.

Pina epitomises the resistance of ordinary Italians, a resistance which is linked to her devout Catholic faith through her close relationship with Don Pietro and her plan to wed her fiancé Francesco in church rather than at the local fascist registry office. Her resistance is not political but is identified with her natural moral goodness, her passionate sense of self and her instinctive defiance of the occupying Germans. These traits establish her as an emblem of Italian womanhood and are reinforced by the lingering image of her lifeless, outstretched body on the street where she is shot – an image which, for Angela Dalle Vacche, typifies Rossellini's subversion of the statuesque fascist body with the 'frail and transitory' (1992: 180) human body of neorealism. Rossellini also emphasises the self-assurance with which communist resistants act. Francesco, who publishes the underground communist newspaper *L'Unità*, reassures Pina that the war will soon end: 'Spring will come, more beautiful because we'll be free ... We mustn't be afraid now or in the future because we're in the right, on the right road.

Fig. 3 Pina defies the occupying Germans in *Rome, Open City*

We're fighting for something that must come. It may be a long hard road but we'll get there and we'll see a new world, our children will see it.' Later, with quiet moral certainty, Don Pietro debates with the outraged SS officer, Major Bergmann, on the morality of occupation and resistance while, in the background, Bergmann's men prepare Manfredi for torture with ropes and a blowtorch. Having refused to talk to his captors, Manfredi's crumpled corpse, like that of Pina, is proposed as a sign of Italian sacrifice – one which fills Don Pietro with sorrow but also admiration as he lashes out at the Germans, 'It's finished! You wanted to kill his soul but you've only killed his body. You're damned. You'll all be trodden into the dust!'

Through these images of stoic endurance, Rossellini begins to build a new mythology of Italian national identity whose humility and humanity contrasts with the bombast and corporatism of the fascist era. *Rome, Open City*, like his next film *Paisà*, has its own nationalist self-assurance as much as any of its fictional characters. Indeed, the view of Italian history projected in these films has often been related to that of Benedetto Croce, the Neapolitan historian and author of the famous *History of Italy from 1871 to 1915* (1928). Croce put forward a highly influential liberal-humanist account of the unification of Italy and its emergence as a modern nation-state, and his idealist perspective led him to regard the rise of fascism as a perverse aberration from the positive course of Italian history. Having published a 'Manifesto of Anti-fascist Intellectuals' in *La critica* on 1 May 1925, he was forced to live out the rest of the fascist era in seclusion in Naples and, after the war, was a national hero for his resistance, especially among Christian Democrats for whom he provided an alternative hero to that of the Communist Party, the Marxist intellectual and writer Antonio Gramsci.

The partnership of resistance and heroic death which the communist, Manfredi, and the Catholic priest, Don Pietro, share in *Rome, Open City* acknowledges the working partnership of communists and Catholics in the actual historical resistance. Indeed, the acknowledgment is also there in the proposed marriage of Pina (Catholic) and Francesco (Communist). Immediately after the war, coalition governments were the order of the day and to many a pragmatic alliance of left and right seemed to offer the best possible route for Italian politics – at least until 1948 when elections put the Christian Democrats in a dominant position not seriously undermined until the 1960s. Whether the film clearly takes one side or the other has long been a subject of debate. P. Adams Sitney (1995: 13), for example, suggests that Rossellini's sympathy leans towards the Catholic: Rossellini viewed neorealism as 'a moral position' and key images in the film identify his morality as Catholic, including the representation of the dead Manfredi as if he was Christ and the final shot of the film in which we see the dome of St Peter's. Catholic iconography is certainly present in *Rome, Open City*, as it is in many neorealist films, and Sitney importantly points out that Rossellini was appointed as a liaison between the film industry and Christian Democrats in 1945. However, the presence of Catholic iconography in the film does not necessarily imply endorsement of Catholicism. *The Miracle* and many of Rossellini's other films met with the harsh disapproval of the Christian Democrats and the Catholic Church itself deemed *Rome, Open City* 'unsuitable for children'. It is fairer to say, therefore, that Rossellini's film pays *equal* attention and tribute to the heroism of the left. Francesco and Giorgio are presented as hard-working activists who have none of the official authority of the Church but are genuinely popular among the people, and who take exceptional risks on their behalf. Don Pietro's death closes the film but that of Giorgio is emphasised for its length and horror and for his refusal to talk, a sign of fidelity to Italy and its people. The film does not lean clearly in one direction or another but suggests a positive and progressive alliance between the two camps, projecting an ideal of a future non-partisan Italy, albeit one which never really came to fruition.

Indeed, the final shot of the film is not a shot of St Peter's as such but an image of the city as a whole. Melodrama, self-absorption and brutality are identified with the interior spaces of Nazi headquarters but the city is identified with liberty and unity. This sense is not only evident in the film's title but in its representation of the city in terms of control and resistance. In the opening sequence, panning shots of nighttime rooftops under curfew and of patrolling German troops, present a city oppressed by an alien force. At Gestapo headquarters, maps identify zones of control. However, much of the action takes place in another realm. Rossellini presents the everyday life of the Roman people as a range of illicit activities: black market trading in bread and cigarettes, people discussing an anticipated arrival of American forces, Don Pietro scurrying through the streets with money or messages hidden in books, Francesco dodging the police on his way to print *L'Unità*. These scenes initiate a common motif in Rossellini's films in which characters navigate urban space as a matter of survival and self-discovery – in *Paisà*, the walks of the US military police officer Joe and the street urchin Pasquale through Naples, or the race across Florence by Harriet as she searches for her lover during battle; the aimless wandering through Berlin of the boy Edmund Koeler in *Germany Year Zero*; the investigation of Naples by Katherine in *Journey to Italy*. In *Rome, Open City*, as in these other films, the city is alive with activity. Rossellini populates the wartorn streets with chatting neighbours and children playing football to emphasise the familial unity of the people. Boys, girls and babies stand as signs of youth and hope. The social landscape abounds with welcome chaos. Everyday noise recalls the 'shout in the street' which Marshall Berman describes as a central characteristic of urban modernity (1983: 312). The density of activity, sight and sound, peaks during the sequence in which German troops round up resistants on Pina's wedding day. Rossellini exploits the bright sunlight of the scene, together with high-angle shots, to accentuate the sense of enclosure felt by the indignant people pinned against a wall, unable to move. Rome, the city, becomes a stand-in for Italy, the nation. The film closes outdoors just as it began, but now the darkness and oppression of the opening sequence is cancelled out by neorealist light and air. As the young boys disappear into its streets, having witnessed Don Pietro's execution, the city appears no longer as a zone of authoritarian control but as a source of inspiration for a people in revolt.

Fig. 4 The final shot of Rome in *Rome, Open City*

This uplifting and unifying motif was at the heart of the film's popular success upon its release in October 1945 and in the United States and France the following year. In Italy, *Rome, Open City* was widely praised by critics of all shades of political opinion, including those of both the Christian Democrat newspaper *Il popolo* and the Communist Party's *L'Unità*. In the latter, Umberto Barbaro argued that the film reproduced the hardships and injustices of the occupation 'with an objectivity lacking in rhetoric and with an implicit political judgement that is judicious and fair, so that the film undoubtedly deserves the praise of all honest men' (quoted in Sitney 1995: 30). Few negative assessments of the film emerged, although Alberto Vechietti, writing in the socialist *Avanti!*, did criticise it for fudging the relationship between Catholicism and the politics of the left. But Vechietti missed the point. *Rome, Open City* achieved a powerful formal *and* ideological reconfiguration of Italian cinema in an invigorating new social context and the broad critical consensus in favour of the film reflected a careful negotiation of the relationship between the key blocs in Italy's post-war political landscape. In later years, that negotiation would prove more and more difficult for neorealists to sustain.

Bicycle Thieves

Bicycle Thieves, the third collaboration between the director Vittorio De Sica and writer Cesare Zavattini, achieves a different kind of balance to Rossellini's *Rome, Open City*. It does not present an alliance of Catholicism and Communism but a merger of metaphysical and political concerns arising out the social and material deprivation and hardship afflicting Italian cities after the war. Unlike *Rome, Open City*, the balance achieved in *Bicycle Thieves* has little to do with institutions – whether church, police or political party. Indeed, only one, relatively short, sequence in the film takes place in a church, another at a local police station, and another in a labour union hall, and there are no figures of imposing authority in any of these places. Instead, *Bicycle Thieves* focuses even more resolutely, and with even less symbolism, than Rossellini's film on ordinary people and their urban environment.

In 1946 De Sica and Zavattini had moved beyond the muted social critique of *The Children Are Watching Us* with *Shoeshine*, a powerful and direct indictment of the brutality and injustice experienced by two orphan shoeshine boys, Giuseppe and Pasquale, who are convicted of handling stolen goods on the black market and committed to a borstal run by inhumane state officials and priests. At the time, De Sica and Zavattini were part of the circle of leftist writer-filmmakers associated with the magazine *Film d'oggi* which included De Santis, Puccini and Amidei. Coming from a background in commercial Italian cinema but deeply shocked by post-war conditions, De Sica equally admired the sentimental comedies of Chaplin and the objectively descriptive, ethnographic documentaries of Robert Flaherty, *Nanook of the North* (1922) and *Man of Aran* (1934). He described the preoccupations of his neorealist films not in terms of concrete political issues but, more abstractly, in terms of a tension in post-war Italian society between 'egoism' and 'solidarity' (see Samuels 1987: 149–50). A sensitivity to this tension united De Sica and Zavattini, although the latter was more comfortable with overtly political descriptions of neorealist cinema as an opposition to what he called 'the capitalistic system of cinema production' and was firmly convinced that 'the cinema should take as its subject the daily existence and condition of the Italian people' (1979: 72). In extensive writings and public statements, Zavattini expounded an idealistic belief in cinema as a means to the understanding of human existence and inter-personal communication, and to the resolution of social problems of ignorance, alienation, injustice and poverty.

Bicycle Thieves was undoubtedly the most celebrated product of the De Sica and Zavattini partnership. Made on a relatively substantial budget of 100 million lire and with a large crew, sometimes filming with multiple cameras, its production was a less rough-and-ready affair than that of *Rome, Open City*. Its narrative was very loosely adapted from a novel by Luigi Bartolini, set in September 1944, which concerned the theft of a bicycle from a man who is an artist and a writer with a rather self-absorbed character and a sense of superiority to the common people. The adaptation kept the premise of the theft but reorganised its narrative around a typical and sympathetic unemployed working-class man who finds work as a bill-poster and who is located firmly within the social milieu of 1948, a year which saw unemployment in post-war Italy peak. The narrative was thin, tightly focused on the man, Antonio Ricci, and his son, Bruno, and containing only one line of action – their search for Antonio's bicycle. In *Aesthetics of Film*, Jacques Aumont and his co-authors argue that that line of action is enough to describe *Bicycle Thieves* as a classical narrative: 'Whether the hero departs in search of his stolen bicycle or attempts to recover an atomic secret that a spy is about to hand over to the enemy, the story still involves a "quest" that follows a "misdeed" that upset the "initial situation"' (Aumont *et al.* 1999: 111). But this argument seriously understates the attenuation of classical narrative structure, active characterisation and narrative closure evident in the film. *Bicycle Thieves* marked a decisive step away from traditional storytelling in favour of the description of tenuously-connected events. Zavattini, in particular, was committed to dissolving classical narrative in a solution of 'life as it is' (quoted in Liehm 1984: 103).

The events which befall Antonio and Bruno as they search Rome for the bicycle are connected only by their search, which is highly unsystematic, and by the bicycle, which is never found. Indeed, the film has no dramatic conflict at all and its protagonists spend as much time wasting time as searching – sheltering in the rain, eating dinner, sitting on the kerb in despair. Only two scenes contain any dramatic action – that is, the two bicycle thefts – and even these are over in the blink of an eye. Bazin declared approvingly of the film's simplicity of plot: 'Plainly there is not enough material here even for a news item: the whole story would not deserve two lines in a stray-dog column' (1971a: 50). Throughout, instead of following a classical narrative, we are invited to observe for the sake of observation as the film's simple premise and plot give way to a complex web of social and metaphysical meanings.

In *Bicycle Thieves*, therefore, the city of Rome is a subject in itself to an even greater degree than it was in *Rome, Open City*. The action takes place primarily out of doors, filmed on location over a wide geographical area. It presents an image of the city comprising everyday streets, tenements, a market, an ordinary church, a trattoria and a football stadium, rather than historical monuments and symbolic spaces. Particular locations can be identified, of course: Antonio's tenement building in the Valmelaina district; his confrontation, on the Ponte Palatino, with an old man he suspects of knowing the thief of his bicycle; his apprehension of a man he thinks is the actual thief in the Via Panico; his searching for his bicycle in the famous Porta Portese market; his sheltering in a tunnel under the Quirinale; and the Ponte Duca d'Aosta where he searches for Bruno, momentarily fearing that the boy has drowned in the Tiber. These identifiable spaces, however, are not deployed for any specific symbolic value but merge with the film's innumerable nameless streets to create an impression of the city's bewildering scale and the difficulties it poses for Antonio and Bruno's search.

The mixture of authenticity and anonymity which characterises the city is matched by a similar mixture in the non-professional actors who play the lead roles. In the early stages of planning for *Bicycle Thieves*, the Hollywood producer David O. Selznick had proposed that, in return for American funding and distribution, De Sica should cast a Hollywood star, preferably Cary Grant. However, De Sica was determined to employ non-professional actors – the first time he had done so – in order to enhance the realism of his film with respect to performance. A factory worker, Lamberto Maggiorani, was cast in the role of Antonio, and Enzo Staiola was cast in the role of the boy, Bruno, because of his natural appearance of innocence and warmth. De Sica used his own experience as an actor to coach these non-professionals on the practicalities of acting while seeking to disturb as little as possible the authentic demeanor, mannerisms and expressions they naturally displayed. He described the non-professional actor as 'raw material that can be molded at will', explaining that it was much easier to achieve a sense of authenticity and spontaneity with a non-professional than with a fully trained actor who must 'forget his profession' when working on a neorealist film (De Sica 1969: 5). This authenticity and spontaneity was especially clear in the role of Bruno whom De Sica uses in the film as a focal point for the emotional highs and lows through which the narrative travels. Indeed, although it is the father's bicycle which is stolen and he who risks arrest to escape poverty, the film presents his predicament, and much of the description of social deprivation, through the point of view of the boy. On the one hand, he is presented as a figure of almost angelic innocence who looks up to and even imitates his father as heroic ideal, dwarfed as he is not only by the enormous material problems he and his father face but also, literally, by the physical environment itself. On the other hand, he is a figure of moral and physical stamina upon whom his father depends: it is Bruno who has a proper job, as pump attendant at a local gas station; it is he who remembers the bicycle's all-important serial number, and it is he who fetches a police officer to rescue his father from an angry crowd near the film's end.

On the face of it, the film's foregrounding of the relationship between father and son might be seen as a relatively conservative move which values the collectivity of the family over the more radical collective potential of the working class, but this interpretation cannot be sustained. The ideal of the stable, productive nuclear family has, historically, been of tremendous importance in Italian culture, traditionally supported by the conservative social values of the Catholic Church and, in the 1920s and 1930s, a central element of fascist ideology. Prior to neorealism, the image of the family carried a generally conservative meaning in Italian cinema. For example, both before and during the fascist era, it was used as a metaphor of the moral integrity and superiority of Italian society as a whole in classical epics such as *Cabiria* and *Scipio Africanus* which presented it as a bastion of Roman civilisation under attack from barbarian hordes. In the films of Camerini, such as *Il signor Max*, the family was presented with less obvious symbolism – indeed, the authenticity and honesty of the working-class family was deliberately contrasted with the superficiality and decadence of its upper-class counterpart – but the intention was comic rather than critical, the unifying corporate structure of fascist society as a whole was emphasised, and there was no danger of family breakdown.

With the release of De Sica's *The Children Are Watching Us*, however, images of the family in distress began to proliferate. That film, like *Ossessione*, showed the destructive effects of illicit sexual desire upon the family and the irreparably broken home would become a key motif of neorealist films for years to come, although usually the result of poverty more than lust. In *Bicycle Thieves*, we find an image of the family which recognises the emotional security it can provide while not reinforcing myths of the family as an ideal form of social organisation and moral anchor. The family seems to function – but only just. It has the semblance of unity, especially in the early part of the film before the theft of the bicycle: the Riccis' tenement home is poor but apparently safe and warm; Antonio helps his weary wife, Maria, carry water from a nearby well; and mother, father and son go together in sorrow to the pawnshop where they exchange a cherished wedding gift of linen for much-needed cash. Once the bicycle is stolen, however, the father/son relationship takes over from the whole family unit, and the film concentrates on the threat posed to the family by the bicycle's loss. The mother, Maria, disappears from the film, along with any sense of home, and the father and son are cast out onto the streets in a kind of homelessness which lingers around them even in the final shot as they give up looking for the bicycle and wander off into the crowded Roman streets to face an uncertain future.

De Sica thus presents poverty as a matter of material shortage and of forced physical displacement. The family is vulnerable, but so are individuals and whole cities. The Riccis are repeatedly presented as victims of a wider social crisis. In the opening sequence, Antonio is just one in a crowd of unemployed men waiting desperately for work. Recently arrived in the city from the countryside, he is typical of the migrant working class of the post-war years and he lives with his family in one of the ill-equipped suburban housing projects built by the fascist regime to house migrants and the urban poor. At the pawnbrokers, the Riccis join a long queue, and their blankets join stacks and stacks of others; at the fortune-teller's, Maria sits patiently with scores of other anxious women; at the market, Antonio and Bruno are surrounded by bicycles of which an unknown number may be stolen, each with its own story to tell. The film thus describes the ubiquity of poverty in post-war Rome, using the simple icon of the (missing) bicycle as an index of the collapse and continuing injustice of an entire social and economic system – a tactic also employed by De Sica in the image of the young boys' horse in *Shoeshine* and of the old man's dog in *Umberto D*. There is an awareness of social inequality rather than just wholesale poverty in the scene in which Antonio and Bruno eat in a trattoria next to a table full of well-fed bourgeoisie. The tracing of Antonio's evolution from worker to thief suggests that all crime may be socially caused by poverty, a fact implicitly recognised by the man whose bicycle Antonio steals but who decides to let him go without pressing charges. In that scene, De Sica acknowledges the solidarity of forgiveness in times of hardship. In others, that solidarity is specifically working class, yet it too is unromanticised: in the crowd of men waiting for work at the employment exchange at the beginning of the film, other men are ready to take Antonio's job if he does not answer the boss who calls his name, but Antonio is warned by a fellow down-and-out; in the basement of the trade union building, we find singing

Fig. 5 Poverty and displacement in *Bicycle Thieves*

rehearsals as well as political meetings in progress, but at least Antonio finds some help in looking for his bicycle where at the church and police station he finds none.

Although De Sica declared that *Bicycle Thieves* was a film concerned with 'those social contradictions which society wants to ignore' and a film 'dedicated to the suffering of the humble', he asserted that realism could never be a matter of 'mere documentation' (1979: 88). The critique of the social and economic conditions of post-war Italian society in the film is not the only level on which meaning can be drawn from it as De Sica also presents a meditation on the human condition, on loneliness and isolation, and on the difficulty of social and private relationships. In his appraisal of *Bicycle Thieves*, Siegfried Kracauer appreciated the film's representation of everyday life in the city as 'an unfixable flow which carries fearful uncertainties and alluring excitements' (1997: 72). For Kracauer, De Sica excels, more than any other neorealist, at the description of the geography of Rome as a maze of narrow streets, bridges and piazzas, by turns empty or swarming with bodies, a space in which life is at its most intense, where terror and stimulation mix uneasily. This relatively abstract set of meanings is allowed by De Sica's film and is particularly evident in the organisation of

Fig. 6 The density of the Roman street in *Bicycle Thieves*

the narrative around the theme of chance – the unlucky theft of the bicycle, Antonio's accidental apprehension of the old man outside the church, the useless predictions of the fortune-teller, Antonio's successful theft of a bicycle scuppered by a threatening crowd which comes out of nowhere. The moral, as opposed to political, ramifications of Antonio's predicament carried particular resonance for French critics such as the Catholic priest Amedée Ayfre, who praised De Sica's work in *Cahiers du cinéma* for its 'phenomenological description' of the philosophical meaning of the existence of people and things in time and space over and above their historical and social context (1985: 185). For Ayfre, the film posed questions about the relationship between free will and pre-determination and focused profoundly on an image of life as a series of absolute moral choices between right and wrong, epitomised in Bruno's shame and Antonio's remorse when caught by the angry crowd. By the end of the film, Antonio has come full circle as far as his material circumstances are concerned (once again he has no bicycle and no job) but he, like Bruno, has developed with respect to his understanding of the world and his place in it. As father and son disappear in the final shot back into the people from whence they emerged, the question of what they will do next is unanswered but that it will involve search and struggle is assured. Thus the metaphysical themes with which *Bicycle Thieves* grapples do not float above its material concerns but are intertwined with them even in the final shot.

In this respect, however, the timing of the release of the film in 1948 was as ironic as it was unfortunate and poignant. *Bicycle Thieves* was a commercial and critical success both in Italy and abroad, widely recognised as De Sica's greatest work and immediately praised as the most important neorealist film since *Rome, Open City*. But 1948 was also the year in which Italy's post-war period of government by broad coalition fell apart and the Christian Democrats gained a new ascendancy at the expense of the left. Internationally, the Cold War began in earnest with Italy a major front sandwiched between American and Soviet spheres of influence. In the United States, De Sica's *Shoeshine* had won a special Academy Award in 1947 and *Bicycle Thieves* went on to win Best Picture in a Foreign Language in 1949, but the virulent anti-communism which would paralyse Hollywood in the 1950s was just setting in. In Italy, critical and official responses to *Bicycle Thieves* were more ideologically polarised than those received by any preceding neorealist film and this polarisation would only intensify in later years. Attacks on neorealism would come from Christian Democrats eager to present what they considered a positive, morale-boosting image of Italy at home and abroad and from a Catholic Church eager to promote good morality and edifying views of family life. Despite its sensitive and compassionate portrayal of the hardships of everyday life faced by ordinary Italians, the Catholic journal, *La Rivista del cinematografo*, advised 'caution' for adult viewers of *Bicycle Thieves*. Meanwhile, neorealism was coming under intensifying threat from Hollywood and a resurgent commercial film industry at home. De Sica underlines his awareness of the gulf between neorealism and Hollywood in *Bicycle Thieves* in the poster of Rita Hayworth which, of all possible images, Antonio is pasting on a wall when his bicycle is stolen.

On the other hand, critics on the left were largely enthusiastic in their support of the film. At a time when Carlo Lizzani was calling for a 'reawakening [of] the spirit of the popular masses' (1948: 91) through neorealist cinema, the Communist Party collaborated with De Sica himself to rally audiences for the film, and Guido Aristarco praised it in *Cinema*, though cautioning that De Sica sometimes fell 'into sentimentalism, into an excessive tenderness' (quoted in Debreczeni 1964: 155). Writing for the Catholic socialist magazine *Esprit*, André Bazin praised De Sica's uncompromising portrait of hardship without neat solutions or happy endings, famously exclaiming in response to its innovative form: 'No more actors, no more story, no more sets, which is to say that in the perfect aesthetic illusion of reality there is no more cinema' (1971a: 60). But perhaps Bazin's more important recognition was his description of *Bicycle Thieves* as 'the only valid Communist film of the whole past decade' (1971a: 51). Bazin was a staunch anti-Stalinist and meant his description to be partly ironic, an oblique reference to what he saw as the simple-minded and misleading tendencies of Soviet socialist realism of the late 1940s. But he nonetheless believed in an important and valuable left-wing beyond Stalinism for whom, although such a sentiment might seem almost incomprehensible to most people today, a film could be both Communist and a work of art of philosophical and human value.

3   NEOREALISM AND THE CITY

The city in neorealism

Generally speaking, the greatest spatial distinction which critics and historians of Italian cinema have focused on has been the relationship of social, political and economic inequality between the urban-industrial and modern north of Italy, above Rome, and the rural-agrarian and feudal south or *mezzogiorno*. After the war, the most influential analysis of the north/south division was provided by Antonio Gramsci, the Marxist political theorist and founding member of the Italian Communist Party, who had been imprisoned by the fascist regime from 1927 until his death in 1937, but whose *Prison Notebooks* began to be published in 1948. Gramsci formulated the north/south relationship as a colonial one in which the northern bourgeoisie profited from the subservience of the south and which could only be overturned by a revolutionary strategic alliance of northern industrial workers and southern peasants. The poverty of the rural south was largely suppressed from public discourse in the fascist era, but in the late 1940s it re-emerged in politics and in neorealist cinema which, given its interest in social crisis and reform, was drawn to the subject in Visconti's *La terra trema*, Germi's *In the Name of the Law*, and Luigi Zampa's *Difficult Years* (*Anni difficili*, 1948). Other films extended the themes of poverty and injustice to other parts of rural Italy, especially Giuseppe De Santis' *The Tragic Hunt* (*Caccia tragica*, 1947) and *Bitter Rice*, and Alberto Lattuada's *The Mill on the Po* (*Il mulino del Po*, 1948).

These films led critics such as Roy Armes to suggest that neorealism was more concerned with 'rural conditions and problems' than it was with 'urban settings' (1971: 127). In truth, however, there was a roughly even split between urban and rural settings in neorealist films. De Santis, Germi, Lattuada and Zampa all had success with rural films but none of them continued as a significant neorealist director after 1949 and some critics alleged that they compromised social critique in their films with light-hearted romanticisations of rural life. Meanwhile, in the work of De Sica, Rossellini and Visconti, urban representations had the edge. De Sica's neorealist films give the impression that he almost never stepped foot in the countryside as *Shoeshine*, *Bicycle Thieves* and *Umberto D* are set in Rome while *Miracle in Milan* and *The Gold of Naples* (*L'Oro di Napoli*, 1954) are set in other metropolises. Indeed, De Sica's urbanism had begun with *The Children Are Watching Us* and continued even when he broke with neorealism in *Stazione Termini* (1953). Rossellini created iconic urban images in *Rome, Open City* and *Germany Year Zero* but *Paisà* and *L'Amore* were split equally between urban and rural scenes and, during the early 1950s, Rossellini left the city in making *Stromboli*, *Francis, God's Jester*, and *The Machine to Kill Bad People* before returning to it in *Europa '51* and *Journey to Italy*. Visconti made, firstly, two rural films, *Ossessione* and *La terra trema*, and then two urban ones, *Bellissima* (1951) and *Senso*. Fellini went from a rural setting in *Variety Lights* to urban settings in *The White Sheik* and *I vitelloni*, then back to rural settings in *La Strada* (1954) and *Il bidone* (1955), and back to an urban setting in *The Nights of Cabiria*. Finally, after his initial rural documentary *Gente del Po* (1943), Antonioni was more at home in the city, from *Nettezza Urbana* (1948) and *Cronaca di un amore* (1950) to *La signora senza camelie* (1953), *I vinti* (1953) and *Le amiche* (1955) and even on the odd occasion his films went into the country it too was a place of industrial anguish, as in *Il grido* (1957).

Antonioni's films explored the physical and psychic encroachment of the urban throughout post-war Italy. *Il grido* tells the story of the downfall of Aldo, a factory worker in the Po valley, who despairs of life when his lover Irma leaves him for another man. The splintering of his family and social circle which leads to his suicide is linked by a slow, brooding cinematographic style to the existentially barren landscape and to the coming destruction of the local community of Goriano by the construction of a modern airport. Of course, this film was made in the late 1950s when neorealism was passing and when the modernisation and urbanisation associated with the so-called 'economic miracle' of the 1960s was visible on the horizon. However, the processes it described were already evident in the years immediately after the war. Most rural neorealist films are inscribed with a sense of the encroaching city: in *Ossessione* the café is a waypoint on a busy trunk road between cities; in *La terra trema* the city is a black hole which lures Sicilian youth from their native land; in *Bitter Rice*, the hard-working silence of the rice fields is disturbed by the insistent tones of boogie woogie on the radio. Each highlights what Fabio Sforzi calls the 'diffusion' (1999: 51) of the urban into the rural which characterised Italian life in the post-war period and which included not only the physical expansion of cities into their immediate surroundings in the creation of suburbs, and the migration of people to the city from dwindling rural communities, but also the expansion of communications, media and transport networks from city to city and from city to country.

In this light, neorealism is recast as a primarily urban creature. Indeed, its urbanism was noted by two of its most important chroniclers, André Bazin and Siegfried Kracauer, who shared an interest in the cinematic city. Discussing *Rome, Open City* and *Paisà*, Bazin was drawn to what he saw as the sympathetic character of the Italian city when placed in front of the camera:

> Here the Italians are at an undoubted advantage. The Italian city, ancient or modern, is prodigiously photogenic. From antiquity, Italian city planning has remained theatrical and decorative. City life is a spectacle, a *commedia dell'arte* that the Italians stage for their own pleasure. And even in the poorest quarters of the town, the coral-like groupings of the houses, thanks to the terraces and balconies, offer outstanding possibilities for spectacle. The courtyard is an Elizabethan set in which the show is seen from below, the spectators in the gallery being the actors in the comedy ... Add to this the sunshine and the absence of clouds (chief enemy of shooting on exteriors) and you have explained why the urban exteriors of Italian films are superior to all others. (1971a: 28–9)

Along similar lines, Kracauer argued that neorealist films such as *Umberto D* were among the best examples of what he called 'cinematic films' – that is, films which took advantage of the unique formal and technical qualities of the cinematic medium and its ability to articulate and analyse 'the flow of life' (1997: 71). This flow was most evident in the street in which the materiality of built space was matched by a density of social interaction: 'The street is in the extended sense of the word not only the arena of fleeting impressions and chance encounters but a place where the flow of life is bound to assert itself' (1997: 72). In the street, cinema could apprehend the relationship between the human subject and his or her physical and social environments with particular insight, and that relationship was most intense in moments of historical crisis such as that of neorealism. As Kracauer put it, 'When history is made in the streets, the streets tend to move onto the screen' (1997: 98).

Indeed, Giuliana Bruno (1993), James Hay (1987) and Angelo Restivo (2002) have placed the city firmly at the centre of their studies of Italian cinema in the silent era, the fascist era and the 1960s, respectively. Their work forms part of the now significant range of scholarship which has focused on the cinematic city internationally where, beyond the Italian case, much attention has been given to such cities as Berlin, London, Paris, New York and Los Angeles (Donald 1999; Ward 2001; Barber 1995; Dimendberg 2004). However, surprisingly little attention has been given to the neorealist representation of the city, no doubt partly because of the conceptualisation of neorealism as Italian national cinema and in terms of regional polarity between northern and southern Italy which re-emerged in the years after World War Two. In addition, the Italian neorealist city does not necessarily lend itself directly to the ways in which most studies of the cinematic city have approached questions of urban modernity in other countries.

Donald Pitkin reminds us that the Italian city must be conceptualised differently to its European counterparts, and certainly to its North American equivalents, because of its peculiar relationship to modernity (1993: 96). In neorealist cinema, the city does not epitomise modernity in the manner we associate with *fin de siècle* Paris, Weimar Berlin or 1940s New York but exists between modernity and the pre-modern, its accumulated layers of ancient, medieval and renaissance history always reminding us of the past rather than thrusting us into the future. As Pitkin points out, it is ironic, if understandable, that most sociological interest in the modern city has focused on northern European cities like Paris, Berlin, London and Amsterdam, given that European urbanism began in Mediterranean Europe. Ancient Rome was a highly urbanised society for centuries before the rise of Paris and London, cities which the Romans themselves founded, and Roman civilisation not only developed advanced technologies of planning, architecture and construction but was adept in the management of large, high-density populations and in the symbolic use of the city as a site of imperial control and popular spectacle. In the medieval and renaissance eras, Italy remained at the forefront of urban development. Its small city-republics, each under authoritarian local rule (the Borgias and Barberini's in Rome, the Estes in Ferrara), were at the vanguard of humanist academic learning and artistic experimentation and of capitalist expansion through mercantile trade. However, the Italian city stagnated in the eighteenth century and, by the height of the Industrial Revolution in the nineteenth, it had fallen behind, hampered by Italy's increasingly peripheral position in southern Europe and its internal division until unification in the 1860s. Even after unification, Italy remained outside the main zone of European urban industrial expansion. By the early twentieth century Britain, the Netherlands, Belgium, Germany and France, had all become urbanised societies in the sense of having more people living in their cities than in the countryside but Italy did not catch up until the 'economic miracle' of the late 1950s and 1960s.

This is one of the reasons the urban society which neorealist cinema presents is often less concentrated and metropolitan than that of other urban-oriented cinemas. We see, in addition to the large cities of Milan, Naples and Rome, a large and well-dispersed range of mid-sized and small cities which reflect what Giuseppe De Matteis has described as the distinctly 'polycentric' (1999: 144) character of Italy's urban system. These non-metropolitan cities feature frequently in neorealist films and are a legacy of its late formation as a nation-state. In Visconti's *Ossessione*, although the primary setting in the Po valley is a rural one, significant parts of the action take place in Ancona, where Gino and the Spaniard dream of bohemian escape, and Ferrara, where Gino and Giovanna fall out over their murder of Bragana. In other films, the setting is not so much a city as a town. In Rossellini's *The Machine to Kill Bad People* Salerno has much of the street life we expect of an urban environment and its narrative revolves around the modern figure of a photographer, but the social fabric of the local community is traditional in the sense of being tightly-knit and the film's opening shot of the Gulf of Salerno makes clear that this is really a large town on the verge of development as a tourist destination. *I vitelloni* presents Fellini's native Rimini as a dead-end town and its young protagonists as layabouts with more restless energy than the town can absorb: in the final scene, the dreamer Moraldo escapes by train for a new life in Rome but it is not at all clear whether his alienation will be dissipated or intensified by the excitement of the big city.

In neorealist cinema, even the metropolises of Rome, Milan and Naples do not, for the most part, display the productive speed, physical energy, sensory intensity and material abundance which characterise urban modernity for cultural historians such as Marshall Berman (1983) and Leo

Charney and Vanessa Schwartz (1995). These qualities had been character-istic of urban-oriented films of the inter-war period as diverse as *Sunrise* (F. W. Murnau, 1927), *Man with a Movie Camera* (Dziga Vertov, 1929), *Hôtel du Nord* (Marcel Carné, 1938), and even the comedies of Mario Camerini, and after the war they would be central to city-themed American musicals such as *On the Town* (Stanley Donen, 1949) and *film noirs* such as *Force of Evil* (Abraham Polonsky, 1948). But they were out of the question in neorealism immediately after the war given the physical destruction of Italian cities, which led to a lack of buildings and infrastructure, and the collapse of the economy, which led to a lack of food and other commodities. In *Paisà*, the challenges faced by residents of Naples and Florence are not existential but material: for them, the problem is not that in the constantly changing environment of the modern city 'all that is solid melts into air', to borrow a phrase from Marshall Berman, but that everything that was solid has literally been turned into rubble. Of course, *Paisà* is an extreme case – one of relatively few neorealist films which spend any length of time among the bombed-out ruins of Italian cities – but *Shoeshine*, *Bicycle Thieves*, *Miracle in Milan* and *Umberto D* demonstrate the social destruction which accompanied the physical and which lingered long after the ruins had been cleared away. Neorealist images of post-war urban crisis are an especially important legacy because Italy was the only one of the defeated Axis powers whose cinematic representations of the city achieved iconic status internationally so soon after its military defeat. Representations of wartorn German cities such as Jacques Tourneur's *Berlin Express* (1948) and George Seaton's *The Big Lift* (1950) were produced by outsiders from Hollywood in the absence of a German film industry which did not recover until the New German Cinema of the 1970s. Cinematic representations of urban Japan such as Kenji Mizoguchi's *Women of the Night* (1948), Akira Kurosawa's *Stray Dog* (1949) and Yasujiro Ozu's *Tokyo Story* (1953), while not uncom-mon in the ten years after the war, did not receive proper international distribution until the 1960s. Meanwhile, in post-war Britain, in feature films such as *Passport to Pimlico* (Henry Cornelius, 1949) and in documentaries such as *Land of Promise* (Paul Rotha, 1946), the moral consolation of vic-tory provided some compensation for the reality of urban destruction.

This is not to say that images of bombed-out European cities were not widespread in the immediate post-war period. As Stephen Barber has explained in *Fragments of the European City*, newsreels in 1945 and 1946 presented mass audiences with detailed accounts of 'the destroyed cities of Europe' which to this day remain 'one of *the* punctuation points in the depiction by film of urban space' (1995: 56). In neorealist cinema, however, the destruction was not only human and physical but also metaphysical and existential. No film in all of post-war cinema managed to blend the documentation of material hardships and the exploration of spiritual trauma to more disturbing effect than Rossellini's *Germany Year Zero*. Its long, brooding tracking shots, combined with a striking score by Renzo Rossellini, powerfully expressed the moral disorientation of the 12-year-old boy Edmund Koeler in a Berlin so flattened by bombs that it was barely recognisable as a city at all. The most interesting feature of Rossellini's film, however, was not its presentation of fallen buildings *per se* but its use of them to characterise Berlin as a chilling moral vacuum in which not even a child can see any hope for the future. The problem for Edmund is that the victory of the Allies appears to have brought little for ordinary Germans except destitution and depression and, despite its military defeat, Nazism lingers in the attitudes of many of his embittered elders. Rossellini uses the image of one of the few imposing edifices left in the city, Hitler's ruined headquarters, the Reichschancellery, as an architectural index of this predicament. While British soldiers kick around among the ruins out of curious disgust, Edmund is sent to the Reichschancellery by his former teacher and Nazi-sympathiser, Herr Enning, to sell a phonograph record of Hitler's speeches in order to buy food. As Hitler's recorded voice screams 'Victory will be ours!!!', the architectural scale of the Reichschancellery still manages to make its presence felt in a sea of rubble through its ghostly yet stubborn fixity. Edmund falls under the spell of Enning's fascist logic that 'the weak perish, the strong survive' and is driven to the murder of his own starving and self-pitying father, then to his own suicide. Unsurprisingly, *Germany Year Zero* was a commercial and critical failure in its day. Rossellini used architecture to imply that that the reconstruction of the European city would be much more than a matter of bricks and mortar alone.

However, *Germany Year Zero* is unusual among neorealist films for featuring a well-known architectural icon in such a central role. Most neorealist films are content to keep such buildings at arm's length. In *Paisà*, the Colosseum in Rome appears only incidentally in the distant background as Fred mounts his truck to join his fellow GIs on the road out of the city, leaving behind his lover Francesca, and Rome itself, disenchanted; later, in Florence, two British officers with binoculars, disengaged from the battle raging around them, admire the city's Duomo and Campanile from the far side of the river Arno. In *Umberto D*, the classical portico of the Pantheon appears as a formless but menacing wall of shadow whose bulk looms over

Umberto as he begs for small change in desperation and shame. Even the dome of St Peter's in *Rome, Open City*, which appears in the horizon of the final shot after the Germans' execution of Don Pietro, is only tentatively symbolic of Rossellini's hope for a better Italy after the war. The deployment of these urban icons is casual and modest. It contrasts clearly with the touristic myths of the Italian city as a place of classical beauty or exotic decadence which had been well-established in Western culture for centuries in everything from Florentine renaissance painting to the nineteenth-century novels of Henry James. It also answers back to the deliberate and bombastic ways in which Italian architecture had been deployed by the fascist regime for which the city and its buildings were a means to project fixed ideological meaning.

The fascist city

As suggested earlier, cinematic representations of the city in the fascist era emphasised urbanisation and modernisation as positive evidence of the providential and productive rule of Mussolini's regime. Films such as Camerini's *The Rails, What Rascals Men Are!* and *Il signor Max* contained a mild critique of social customs but wrapped these up in a presentation of Italy as an essentially contented and orderly modern, urban society. This lent credibility to the fascist regime's belief in ambitious projects of urban (re-)construction as a means of symbolic expression. Although Italian fascism relied greatly on rural support in its early years, in the 1930s it turned more attention to the urban middle class and placed the city at the centre of its social and political agendas and its symbolic vocabulary. Mussolini was repeatedly associated with public works of urban construction through newsreels and press accounts of his visits to building sites across Italy and with older urban icons, connoting Italian nobility and martial history, such as the Altare della Patria (1911), a statue to King Vittorio Emmanuele II in the Piazza Venezia in Rome. Taking its cue from the devotion to urban modernity and the heroic speed of the machine age which had characterised Italian Futurism in art, literature and architecture prior to World War One – for example, in the paintings of Umberto Boccioni and the building projects of Antonio Sant'Elia – the regime's sense of the need for the city to be organised as an efficient modern living space and site of symbolic power fuelled a reorganisation of Italian cities from the mid-1920s to the early 1940s. The discipline of *urbanistica*, the profession and study of urban planning, was officially recognised with the 1930 foundation of the

Istituto Nazionale di Urbanistica, which was intended to legitimise fascist policies among Italian architects and planners who were needed to achieve the fascist agenda of urban social and architectural re-engineering.

Bologna, Naples and Milan experienced significant urban reconstruction in the 1920s and 1930s, but fascist attention focused on Rome because it was the capital and the largest city and because its particularly rich associations with the glory of ancient Rome suggested the city to the fascists, as Robert Fried puts it, as a natural symbol of national 'pride, power and discipline (1973: 31). The restructuring of the city under fascism was typified by what Richard Etlin calls 'monumental axial planning' (1990: 393), an approach first outlined in grand plans for Rome drawn up for the regime by Marcello Piacentini in 1925 and 1931. Mussolini moved government offices around Rome in order to centralise the Piazza Venezia as the city's and the nation's seat of government. Programmes of demolition known as *sventramenti* widened streets and made way for modern buildings within the city's tapestry of ancient, medieval, renaissance and baroque buildings and spaces. The creation of the via dell'Impero (now the via dei Fori Imperiali) provided a new space for grand military parades and state occasions, while the cutting of the Via della Conciliazione, which demolished the old neighborhoods of the Borgo Vecchio and the Borgo Nuovo in front of St Peter's, removed some of what many fascists considered the unattractive clutter of the city's historical centre and symbolised the reconciliation of Church and State in the 1929 Lateran Pact. The displacement caused by these works was absorbed by a relaxation in the maximum height of residential buildings allowed in Rome and by mass relocations of inner-city communities to new, purpose-built suburban accommodation of the type planned for the reclaimed Pontine marshes featured in Blasetti's *Sole*.

As in cinema, there was no attempt by the fascist regime to enforce one particular architectural style but virtually nothing was built which did not contribute to its imperatives for the Italian city and the corporate state. In fact, an effort was made by the regime to incorporate current architectural styles in the name of its greater glory in a manner parallel to its incorporation of realism in cinema as a means of self-legitimisation. As the fascist state appealed to every Italian to rise above the limited interests of their private self and class, so it appealed to Italian architects and urban planners to work on its behalf and, thereby, that of Italy. The 'Manifesto of Fascist Intellectuals' published by Giovanni Gentile in April 1925 seduced as many of these to the fascist cause as it did filmmakers and none more so than the members of Italy's leading modernist architectural avant-garde Gruppo

7. Favoring simple functional forms in concrete for which their architecture became known as 'rationalism' (*razionalismo*), this group adapted the principles of Le Corbusier's *Vers une architecture* (1923) and Walter Gropius' *Internationale Architektur* (1925), principles which they articulated in the journal *Casabella*. It enthusiastically welcomed the fascist reorganisation of the Italian city along what were seen as the enviable modern lines of Paris or New York. In a political error of gigantic proportions, its members interpreted fascism as a young and dynamic revolutionary movement which was working to improve Italian society and which could serve as a vehicle for innovative architecture. In 1928 and 1931, with the First and Second Italian Exposition of Rational Architecture, both held in Rome, the rationalists courted the fascist regime and were rewarded by numerous commissions for residential and public buildings. Some of these, such as Mario Ridolfi's post office building in the Piazza Bologna, Rome (1933) and Giuseppe Terragni's Novocomum apartments, Como (1929) might be thought of as the architectural equivalents of Mario Camerini's comedies – formally innovative but within parameters set by the regime. Others, such as Terragni's Casa del Fascio (1932–6), which served as the local fascist party headquarters in Como, and Adalberto Libera and Mario De Renzi's exhibition hall for the 1932 Mostra della Rivoluzione Fascista, might parallel the more forthright ideological posturing of Blasetti's *Sole* and *The Old Guard*.

However, the co-optation of modernist architecture by the fascist regime reached a low point with the work of rationalist architects for the Esposizione Universale Roma (EUR) of 1942. Sometimes known simply as E42, this was the *Scipio Africanus* of Italian architecture and planning under fascism. Its origins lay in Piacentini's axial plans for Rome which proposed a coordinated arrangement of specialised 'cities' on the outskirts, each of which would be an extensive campus of buildings dedicated to a particular area of activity. E42 thus followed the Città dello sport (begun 1928), the Città universitaria (1935), the Città militare and the Città del cinema (Cinecittà, 1937). As Etlin explains, E42, like its forerunners, matched scale and ambition in urban planning with the 'colossal and massive forms' favoured by the regime for their expression of fascism's 'combative aspects' and its 'privileged nationalism' (1990: xvi). The largest project undertaken during the fascist era, E42 was planned to be the venue of the largest world fair in history, to eclipse those of Chicago in 1933 and Paris in 1937, which the regime planned to organise around the theme of 'Twenty-Seven Centuries of Civilisation', explicitly linking fascist Rome with

Fig. 7 Giuseppe Terragni, Casa del Fascio, Como, 1932–6

the foundation of ancient Rome in the seventh century BC. For Mussolini, it was always conceived as an expression of empire in its historical references, its sheer scale, and in its situation to the west of Rome on the via del Mare which led to the Mediterranean sea, the literal and symbolic source of the might of modern Italy and of ancient Rome.

Architectural neorealism

Fascist-era architecture is largely absent from neorealist films but is sometimes used to effect. In *Rome, Open City*, Rossellini undercuts the fascist symbolism of the EUR by unceremoniously displacing one of its most prominent buildings, the Palazzo della Civiltà del Lavoro (1938–43), to the distant horizon while resistance fighters heroically ambush a German convoy in the foreground. Visconti's *Bellissima* was filmed partly at Cinecittà and its critique of the vanity and vulgarity of popular movie culture may be said to extend also to a critique of the architecture of the studios themselves. De Sica's *Miracle in Milan* makes architectural distinctions between the makeshift homes of the tramps on the city's outskirts and the ornate neoclassical offices of the greedy property developer Mobbi which bear an uncanny resemblance to Il Duce's Gymnasium at the Foro Mussolini, designed and built by Luigi Moretti in 1937. Apart from these, however, neorealist cinema largely ignores fascist architecture. Its images of the city seek to undo the fascists' work of ideological investment in architecture and planning in keeping with the post-war reorientation of the discipline of *urbanistica* as a whole.

Even at the height of rationalist architects' cooperation with the fascist regime, architectural traditionalists condemned them as communist or Jewish infiltrators and by the early 1940s it was clear that rationalism was being overtaken by a vulgar and propagandistic form of monumental classicism. In 1943, just before the regime's collapse, the rationalist journal *Casabella* was banned and many rationalists joined the anti-fascist underground. Several were arrested and persecuted, including Giuseppe Pagano who died at Mauthausen concentration camp in Germany on 22 April 1945. After the war, a sense of guilt was widespread among architects such as Ernesto Rogers who survived and continued to work, and this combined with a new sense of creative liberty among architects and planners to inspire a break with the practices of fascism. As Agnoldomenico Pica has put it, in architecture just as much as in cinema, 'it was easy to speak in apocalyptic terms of "Year Zero"' in 1945 (1959: xix). Given the physical destruction of Italian cities, towns and infrastructure, architects, planners, engineers and builders faced unprecedented challenges to rebuild as much and as quickly as possible. Factories, roads, railways, ports, schools, hospitals and utilities had to be reconstructed. In journals such as *Domus* and *Urbanistica*, the best solutions to the country's problems were earnestly debated. Architectural triennales were held in Milan in 1947, 1951, 1954 and 1957. Schools of architecture were expanded under new leadership, such as that of Ernesto Rogers in Milan and Pier Luigi Nervi in Rome, and architectural historians such as Bruno Zevi and Roberto Pane gradually revised Italian architectural history to correct for the ideological biases of fascism. As much as in Italian cinema, the late 1940s and 1950s became a period of conflict and debate over the future of the Italian city. Where in cinema conflict raged between neorealism and profit-oriented filmmaking as popular entertainment, in relation to the city conflict raged between leftist and free-market models of urban development. The former prioritised social housing, environmental manageability and ethical architecture, while the latter prioritised industrial rebuilding, corporate expansion and a rapid return to economic profitability. For architectural historians such as Pica (1959), Peter Rowe (1997) and Manfredo Tafuri (1989), the leftist tendency was in the ascendancy in the late 1940s and, like the best cinema of the

Fig. 8 Cover of *Urbanistica*, vol. 18, no. 2, Sep–Oct 1949

day, it too was 'neorealist' in its social orientation, philosophical reflection and sense of moral responsibility.

As Tafuri has explained, 'neorealist' architecture was allied to the anti-fascist politics of the Resistance and neorealist architects such as Ludovico Quaroni and Mario Ridolfi were convinced of the urgent need for 'an encounter with active politics' (1989: 3) in their work. This could best be met by prioritising Italy's most practically and symbolically important architectural problem of the post-war period – the shortage of housing. This was a critical problem for the large numbers of people made homeless by the war, but also for the inner-city working-class communities displaced by fascist planning to slums, or *borgate*, on the outskirts of Italy's major cities, and for the thousands after the war who chose to migrate from rural poverty to what they hoped would be a better life in the city. Rowe estimates that in Rome, by 1951, almost seven per cent of the population was living homeless or in temporary accommodation, and a further 22 per cent in unacceptably crowded conditions. Italy's housing crisis was central to the representation of the city in neorealist cinema – in Rossellini's haunting image in *Paisà* of destitute families living in caves outside Naples in filthy conditions akin to those of the real-life caves of Matera which caused a national scandal in the early 1950s; in De Sica's depiction of the overcrowded conditions faced by workers and their families in the tenements of the Roman suburb of Valmelaina in *Bicycle Thieves*; and in Cabiria's physical and metaphorical isolation in the borgata of San Francesco in Acilia outside Rome in Fellini's *The Nights of Cabiria*. The neorealist architecture of Quaroni and Ridolfi, and of the publicly-funded housing authority INA-Casa (1949–56), sought to relieve such conditions. Their project for the Quartiere Tiburtino (begun 1950) exemplified the neorealist focus on low-rise, functional housing built on low-cost marginal land and articulated ideals of social cohesion by harking back to the vernacular style of *mezzogiorno* village construction.

Such ideals were particularly meaningful given the sense of social and then psychic instability which was a natural consequence of the physical destruction of the Italian city. As Barber has argued, 'the dominant human and architectural fixation of European cinema [in the postwar period] became that of displacement' (1995: 62). The protagonists of both *Bicycle Thieves* and *The Nights of Cabiria* are confronted daily with the problem of commuting long distances between the core and periphery of Rome – Antonio and Bruno Ricci have the luxury of a streetcar, but Cabiria, when unable to hitch a ride with a friend, is forced to walk for miles on foot. The latter film, in particular, testifies to the persistent time-lag after World War

Fig. 9 Architectural neorealism: Ludovico Quaroni and Mario Ridolfi, Quartiere Tiburtino, Rome, 1949–54

Two between the physical expansion of Italian suburbs and the development of adequate public transport. It also points to the blurring of the line between city and country effected by the suburban redevelopment of the *borgate* into fully-serviced, modern residential communities. While the post-war Italian countryside was increasingly affected by new forms of subliminal urbanisation and the city centre was turned upside down by the destruction of war, life in the in-between spaces of the suburbs was also a new regime. Although the *quartieri* (neighborhoods) of Italian cities had historically been, and continued to be, more socio-economically mixed than those of cities in other western countries, after World War Two many Italian cities experienced new degrees of social segregation. Indeed, Tafuri has argued that displacement became the norm for large sections of the working class who were disproportionately housed in the margins while the historical centres of cities became increasingly concentrated as the preserve of the bourgeoisie, a process which accelerated with the 'economic miracle' of the late 1950s and 1960s (1989: 43). In this context, neorealist architecture responded not only to the urgent practical need for innovative housing solutions but also to the psychological need for solidarity.

However, here we need to recall the distinction made in the introduction between the overlapping first and second phases of neorealism – the first from 1943 to 1950 and the second from 1950 to 1957. Neorealist films of the first phase nearly always make an effort to present the predicaments and challenges faced by their protagonists as typical of society as a whole. *Rome, Open City* insists upon the solidarity of the Italian people in resistance to German occupation. Giuseppe and Pasquale in *Shoeshine* are closely bonded not only to each other as friends but to the community of boys they hang out with on the streets of Rome and in the reformatory to which they are sent for handling stolen blankets. The opening scene of *Bicycle Thieves* situates Antonio Ricci as just one out-of-work Roman among many waiting desperately outside an employment exchange, while in the final shot he and his son, Bruno, disappear anonymously back into the hurrying crowds. Toto, the protagonist of *Miracle in Milan*, begins as a naïf whose bag of personal possessions is snatched almost as soon as he arrives in the city before he finds a home in a shanty town where De Sica emphasises the good-natured camaraderie and sense of humour which unites the homeless in their misery. The protagonists of all of these films share the experience of hardship and displacement which was the common lot of so many Italians in the first years after the war.

However, during the 1950s, a subtle shift of emphasis occurs from solidarity to disconnection in the relationship between the protagonist of the neorealist film and his or her urban milieu. In *Bellissima*, *I vitelloni*, *The Gold of Naples* and *The Nights of Cabiria*, we see signs of Italian city life returning to the normal routines and material comforts of peacetime. Italian society is no longer one in which austerity breeds community – instead, increasing affluence breaks it down. *Bellissima* exposes the self-centered vanity which popular film encourages among its fans. *I vitelloni* offsets the lazy hedonism of its young characters against the hard-working but conformist monotony of their parents whose values they do not share. The first two episodes of *The Gold of Naples* present images of happy and frenetic Neapolitan family life in which the city is a place of 'love of life, patience and eternal hope', but then this touristic vision is demolished in the second two episodes which focus on the sense of entrapment which torments the compulsive gambler, Count Prosper B, and Theresa, the prostitute forced into an arranged marriage to a man still in love with his dead first wife. These neorealist protagonists remain members of society but their experiences are no longer so closely related to the mass of the Italian populace. The crises through which they live are more private and the mode of their cinematic depiction more reflective. As will be explained in chapter five, no film more than Antonioni's *Cronaca di un amore* encapsulates the expansion of neorealism to incorporate representations of the bourgeoisie and bourgeois architectural environments whose excessive artificiality, lack of human content and suffocating luxury are a source of anguish. The alienating buildings and spaces of cosmopolitan Milan which fascinate Antonioni witness the disheartening eclipse of neorealist architecture and planning in the 1950s by a resurgent rationalism in austere residential high-rises and streamlined corporate offices and factories but now backed by big business rather than by fascism. Thus the shift between phases of neorealist film history is paralleled in the history of neorealist architecture. As Vittorio Gregotti has explained, beginning with the 1948 general election victory of the Christian Democrats over the combined forces of the Socialist and Communist parties, neorealist architects experienced 'disappointment at the failure of their hopes for a progressive transformation of the entire socio-political structure' (1968: 46). Neorealism in architecture was forced onto the defensive by a growth in private sources of investment and an increasingly individualistic vision of society. INA-Casa limped on into a second phase of home-building (1956–63) but with none of its original idealism and coherence. Large-scale, steel-frame construction in reinforced concrete overtook the vernacular language of the Quartiere Tiburtino and its village-like model of urban planning was wiped out by urban sprawl, especially in Rome and Milan.

The material conditions which kick-started neorealism in both architecture and film were the same and the intellectual and moral concerns which fuelled their evolution mirrored one another. Tafuri likens the overtaking of neorealist architecture and planning by corporate capitalism to the progression from *Rome, Open City* to commercial Italian films of the mid-1950s such as Luigi Comencini's *Bread, Love, and Dreams* (*Pane, amore, e fantasia*, 1953) (1989: 19). In the second phase of neorealist cinema, its struggle with commercial filmmaking intensified. Its own mass-market spin-offs *neorealismo rosa* and *commedia all'italiana* combined with the market power of Hollywood to marginalise it and force it through a series of formal and thematic transformations. Those transformations led many to proclaim neorealist cinema dead but others to champion its self-conscious and creative adaptation. The battle between these camps will form the subject of the next chapter.

4   THE BATTLE OF NEOREALISM

Neorealism and the Left

Immediately after World War Two, the Italian left was in a strong position. The heroic struggle of its partisans had been key to the anti-fascist resistance and was held in high esteem. A large section of the people – especially the young, men, the urban working class and farm labourers in northern and central Italy – saw the Communists and Socialists as agents of progressive social change, a view reflected in the 1946 elections in which the combined vote of the PCI (18.9 per cent) and PSI (20.7 per cent) exceeded that of the DC (35.1 per cent) (see Sitney 1995: 59). The Italian Communist Party was the strongest in Western Europe with widespread influence in the everyday life of urban and rural communities. The intellectual appeal of Marxism was evident in the popularity of Gramsci, in novels by Cesare Pavese, Vasco Pratolini and Italo Calvino, and in the work of neorealist filmmakers – especially those such as Visconti, De Santis and Lizzani, who were clearly leftist. The writer Elio Vittorini in 1947 explained why he joined the PCI by pointing to the idealistic political commitment of its members:

> They were the best of all people I had known: better in daily life, the most honest, the most serious, the most sensitive, the most dedicated, and at the same time, the happiest and most vivid. That is why I joined the Communist Party: to be with the only ones who were good and courageous, not dejected, not empty; to be with the only ones who had already (in 1941 and 1942) fought for and believed in their struggle; to be with the only ones who, when they reasoned, reasoned as revolutionaries. (1979: 44)

Vittorini, like many of his peers, was critical of what he saw as the cultural and political stagnation of the West but argued for a more humane form of communism for Italy than that of Stalin's Soviet Union. It was an idealistic Marxism which influenced neorealist filmmakers, including left-liberals such as Rossellini and De Sica. Both leftists and left-liberals believed in the potential of cinema to transform society but remained wary of neat party lines and easy solutions to social problems in their films. In the first few years after the war, when neorealism was clearly connected to a leftist politics by a concern with the experience of ordinary people on the level of the street, its films intended or implied a critique of power and injustice in the capitalist society which replaced fascism but which brought little but superficial social and political change. Giuseppe De Santis argued that 'The current Italian cinema is taking part in a long and difficult struggle for a new, civil and modern Italy' (1979b: 218).

Where *Rome, Open City* presented an alliance of communists and Catholics, an explicitly leftist neorealism was announced just one month after the release of Rossellini's film in *Giorni di gloria* (*Days of Glory*, 1945) which also studied the everyday hardships of the occupation, but paid more attention to the actual fighting and purging of fascists which ended it. Filmed around Rome in a documentary style and using newsreel footage, it was scripted by the Marxist Umberto Barbaro and consisted of episodes directed by Visconti, De Santis and Marcello Pagliero (who had played Manfredi in Rossellini's film). It was followed by *Il sole sorge ancora* (1946), directed by the former partisan Aldo Vergano (1891–1957). Vergano had worked as a journalist in the 1920s but, being a critic of the fascist regime, especially after the assassination of the Socialist leader Giacomo Mateotti in 1924, had been forced to leave the profession, entering motion pictures by co-scripting Blasetti's *Sole* and then writing commercially-oriented melodramas and romances for the screen. Co-scripted by the Marxist critic Guido Aristarco, with De Santis and Carlo Lizzani, *Il sole sorge ancora* was partly funded by the Italian Partisan Organisation and was filmed on location with a mixture of professional actors and local people in rural Lombardy. The film told the story of a young soldier, Cesare, who returns home to his family and civilian life in the village of Villavecchia shortly after the fall of Mussolini, where he quickly becomes sympathetic to the partisan cause as the local community is terrorised by occupying German forces and betrayed by local middle-class collaborators. Like Rossellini's *Rome, Open City*, Vergano's film gave a central narrative role to an ad hoc alliance between the local Catholic priest and Communist fighters but unlike Rossellini's film it closed with a relatively conventional action sequence in which local partisans and peasants mount a successful armed revolt which drives the German troops from the town.

In 1948, Visconti directed *La terra trema*, his first feature since *Ossessione*. An adaptation of Verga's *I Malavoglia*, it examined the exploitation of impoverished Sicilian fishermen by an unjust economic system. Inspired by Gramsci, and commissioned by the PCI, Visconti explained that his political aim was to draw attention to the south as 'a great social rupture and as a market for a colonialist type of exploitation by the ruling classes of the North' (quoted in Armes 1971: 107–8). The film was intended to be part of a trilogy which would also focus on disenfranchised farm workers and sulphur miners in southern Italy but which was never finished. Filmed on location with a cast of non-professional actors from the local population, and in a visual style which used slow panning shots and extreme depth of field to relate the fishermen to the harsh natural environment, it has been recognised as one of the most artistically sophisticated examples of neo-realism. However, it was a box-office disaster, dogged by allegations that Visconti allowed Verga's poetic fatalism to overcome his Marxist optimism, by the distributors' attempted cutting of the film against Visconti's wishes, and by their insistence that a dubbed Italian voice-over commentary be added to the film's naturalistic Sicilian dialogue.

The films of De Santis took a different direction in blending Marxist analysis of social problems with action, sex and romance reminiscent of American cinema. De Santis had been one of the first to call for a new cinematic naturalism in the journal *Cinema* in 1941. After co-scripting *Ossessione* and a spell in the anti-fascist resistance, he made his directorial debut in an episode of *Giorni di gloria*. His first feature, *The Tragic Hunt*, was a rousing drama of conflict between a farmers' collective and a gang of bandits which was co-scripted with Lizzani, Puccini, Barbaro and Antonioni and which made significant use of long tracking shots of the wartorn Italian landscape. His *Bitter Rice* was one of the most financially successful neo-realist films. It presented a sympathetic and moving account of the physical and mental hardships of life for women rice workers in the Po valley, emphasising degrading labour conditions and the existential relationship between the laborer and the rural landscape. Its representation of agriculture merged the detailed observation of documentary with a *mise-en-scène* which was epic in scale, overshadowed by foreboding thunderstorms, and often heavily choreographed, especially in its dance sequences and in the gunfight which closed its narrative action. The film demonstrated De Santis's interest in bringing critical messages to a popular audience by employing generic elements from commercial cinema. This was a well-intentioned strategy but a risky one: the late 1940s saw the expansion of a mainstream Italian film industry focused on the production of escapist films and supported by government figures hostile to neorealism and its critical function. De Santis was accused by critics in the Communist Party newspaper *L'Unità* of going too far in his use of Hollywood-style sensationalism, especially in the eroticised representation of the film's star Silvana Mangano. De Santis countered that it was his intention to use Mangano's sensuality not for box-office success at any price but in order 'to express man, woman and society in their ... natural primitive integrity' (quoted in Armes 1971: 130).

It was also the avowed intention of Pietro Germi to bring socially-committed films to mainstream audiences. His *In the Name of the Law* focused on a heroic young magistrate fighting the Sicilian Mafia on behalf of local peasants while *The Path of Hope* (Il cammino della speranza, 1950) dramatised the emigration of Sicilian miners to France in search of a better life. Both films drew attention to working-class oppression and were commercially successful, but both were also accused of diluting neorealism with the influence of the Hollywood Western in their emphasis on the epic landscape of Sicily as a site for action-oriented conflicts of good and evil. Such criticisms, like those of De Santis, highlighted an important difficulty faced by all politically committed filmmakers – how to strike the right balance between political agitation and entertainment.

Neorealism and the Right

As the difficulties encountered by explicitly leftist neorealism suggest, the commercial performance of neorealist films, like their critical reception, was closely entangled in the ideological climate of the day. *Rome, Open City* kept its politics muted but achieved a combination of commercial success and critical acclaim in a moment of unusual anti-fascist consensus which made it number one at the Italian box-office in 1945–6. Vergano's *Il sole sorge ancora* and Visconti's *La terra trema* were more overt in their political committment but, while the former achieved some success as the twelfth highest grossing film of 1946–47, the latter was a terrible commercial failure, grossing only 38m lire in 1948–49 when the most successful film of the year, Raffaello Matarazzo's melodrama *Catene*, took in 735m lire (see Vitti 1996: 40). Germi's *In the Name of the Law* and De Santis' *Bitter Rice* compromised their politics in the name of popular entertainment and were much more commercially successful achieving third place in 1948–49 and fifth place in 1949–50, respectively (see Spinazzola 1985: 18). De Sica's *Bicycle Thieves*, despite the legendary aura which soon came to surround it, was slightly less commercially successful than the films of Germi and De Santis, placed eleventh at the box office in 1948–49, and its critical reception testified to deepening political divisions.

Indeed, the governments by coalition of Communists, Socialists and Christian Democrats in the first few years after 1945 were always full of tension. The PCI, under Palmiro Togliatti, was committed to constitutional, rather than revolutionary, politics but with the outbreak of the Cold War conservative Italian interests, backed by the United States and Britain, played up fears of a Communist incorporation of Italy into the emerging Eastern bloc. In increasingly polarised conditions, neorealism was supported by leftist politicians, artists, intellectuals and film critics, while the Italian business community, the Christian Democrats and the Catholic Church grew increasingly hostile towards it. Neorealists struggled to find a space between two restrictive aesthetics: on the one hand, the escapist, entertainment-oriented cinema which quickly recovered in the late 1940s with the return of Hollywood films to Italy and the rejuvenation of Italy's own commercial cinema; on the other hand, the so-called 'socialist realism' which had become the official style of all visual arts in the Soviet Union since the 1930s, but which aimed primarily at the heroic celebration of the Soviet state (see Bown 1998; Fer *et al.* 1993). As the Cold War intensified, space between these became more and more difficult to find. Filmmakers such as Visconti, Germi and De Santis, who wore their politics too clearly on their sleeves, were the first to be marginalised by official hostility and increasing ideological conformism.

The commercial Italian film industry rebounded, especially with the reopening of Cinecittà in 1948 and the return of genre films – comedies such as Mario Monicelli's *Totò Looks for a House* (*Totò cerca casa*, 1949), blockbuster Roman epics such as Alessandro Blasetti's *Fabiola* (1949) and melodramas such as Raffaello Matarazzo's *Nobody's Children* (*Il figli di nessuno*, 1951). From a low figure of 27 in 1945, the number of feature films produced in Italy each year grew steadily to 67 in 1947, 104 in 1950, 148 in 1952 and 201 in 1954 (see Quaglietti 1980: 44; Brunetta 1995: 14). Although unemployment remained high, real income increased and there was significant growth in the number of cinemas per capita and in the total number of cinema tickets sold, which grew rapidly from 411m in 1946 to 700m in 1952, reaching an all-time peak of 819m in 1955 (see Wagstaff 1996: 147–8).

A battle for control of the Italian film industry broke out even before the end of the War. In 1944, discussions had taken place between the main political parties and filmmakers, leading to the establishment of the Sindacato Lavoratori del Cinema (Film Technicians' Union), while in 1945 film producers established the Associazione Nazionale Industrie Cinematografiche ed Affine (National Association for the Cinema and Related Industries) to lobby the Italian government for protection against Hollywood imports. The United States initially denied an Italian film industry even existed. US Rear Admiral Emery W. Stone, a military administrator during the liberation, declared that 'The so-called Italian film industry was invented by the fascists, therefore it has to be suppressed ... Anyway, Italy is an agricultural country. What would she need a film industry for?' (quoted in Quaglietti 1974: 5). In reality, however, Hollywood control of the post-war Italian film market was overwhelming as the country was flooded by a backlog of films built up since Mussolini excluded Hollywood in 1938, and even at the height of neorealism in 1948 American films commanded 75 per cent of the Italian box office (see Sorlin 1996: 84). In that year, of the total of 464 films which were released in the Italian market, 344 were imported from the United States, 54 were Italian productions and 66 came from Britain, France and elsewhere (see Quaglietti 1980: 245). Successive Italian governments took steps to protect the domestic film industry with tariffs and quotas but Hollywood's market share remained very substantial through the 1950s, fluctuating between a high of 69.2 per cent in 1955 and a low of 53.1 per cent in 1958 (see Quaglietti 1980: 248). Politically, resistance to Hollywood was made difficult by the reliance of Italy's post-war recovery on the United States – $2.2bn of aid and loans from 1943 to 1948 and a further $1.5bn of Marshall Plan finance between 1948 and 1951. This aid, Hollywood's cultural influence, and Italian membership of NATO (after 1949) brought the country more and more firmly within an American sphere of influence.

This was welcomed by big business, landowners, the Catholic Church and Christian Democrats, with the Church threatening to excommunicate communists and anyone who voted for them, and all parties concerned playing on popular fears of a leftist *coup d'état* and supporting armed repression of leftist political organising. In the 1948 elections, the Christian Democrats dramatically beat the combined vote of the Communists and

Socialists, 48.5 per cent to 31 per cent, to achieve a new dominance which would have real effects on neorealism (see Clark 1996: 328; Mafai 2001: 6). The relationship between the Catholic Church and the PCI became terribly antagonistic – the Church had traditionally disapproved of the often salacious content of Hollywood films but was even more worried by neorealism. Its journal, *La Rivista del cinematografo*, condemned *Bitter Rice* outright and advised caution for adult viewers of *Il sole sorge ancora*, *In the Name of the Law*, *La terra trema*, *Bicycle Thieves* and *Umberto D*. Church pressure coincided with that of the Christian Democrat government. Ever since 1946, Christian Democrats had been urging neorealists to produce more edifying representations of Italy. In the 'Andreotti Law' of 1949, named after Undersecretary of Public Entertainment, Giulio Andreotti, these calls were backed up by law, making production loans conditional upon the approval in advance of scripts or story treatments, and reserving for the State the right to require changes in script and casting and the right to block exhibition or export of any film which might harm Italy's national image at home or abroad. The Andreotti Law spearheaded conservative pressure on filmmakers to turn to less politically and artistically challenging cinema, and sought to drive a wedge between commercially-minded producers and creative personnel such as directors, actors and technicians. Many filmmakers protested, a Movement for the Defense of Italian Cinema was established as early as February 1948, and De Santis, De Sica, Germi, Lattuada, Visconti, Zampa and even Blasetti published statements in the Communist journal *Rinascita* expressing their outrage (see De Santis, Germi and Visconti 1979a).

But the stigmatising of neorealism continued. In the Christian Democrat weekly *Libertà*, in February 1952, Andreotti launched a notorious attack on De Sica and his film *Umberto D*, calling for 'a healthy and constructive optimism' in Italian cinema and arguing that De Sica must 'assume his social responsibility, which cannot be limited to a description of the poverty and abuses of a system and of a generation but which must help to overcome them' (quoted in Quaglietti 1974: 37). Andreotti's position made business sense for many producers and investors in the film industry. In truth, however, a certain tendency in neorealism was already producing films which were relatively light-hearted and commercially-oriented. Luigi Zampa's *To Live in Peace* (*Vivere in pace*, 1946) mixed the serious subject of German occupation of a northern Italian mountain village with a comedy of villagers and escaped US prisoners-of-war while emphasising the quaintness rather than hardship of rural life. Alberto Lattuada's *Without Pity* (*Senza pietà*,

1948) centered on a romance between Angela, a young woman driven to prostitution, and Jerry, an African-American GI, against the backdrop of Livorno, the main port for Allied forces, and a mixture of black market crime, car chases and gun fights. With the Christian Democrat victory of 1948, the populist form known as *neorealismo rosa* seemed to give expression to a 'healthy and constructive optimism' by incorporating strong elements of conventional romance and comedy while remaining neorealist in visual style (filmed on location in humble rural or urban settings). André Bazin, while praising *Bicycle Thieves* in his review of the film in 1948, felt compelled to lament the 'emergence of a neorealist superspectacle' in lesser films such as *In the Name of the Law* and *To Live in Peace* 'in which the search for real settings, action taken from everyday life, portrayals of lower-class milieux, social backgrounds, became an academic stereotype' (1971b: 48). In such films, Bazin worried, 'The closed in countryside has replaced the open city' (ibid.).

Similarly, films by Renato Castellani such as *Sotto il sole di Roma* (*Under the Sun of Rome*, 1948), *È primavera* (1949) and *Two Cents' Worth of Hope* (*Due soldi di speranza*, 1951) acknowledged poverty but emphasised a sense of a happy and growing Italy despite it, overwhelming social study with romance. Like Luciano Emmer's *Sunday in August* (*Una Domenica d'agosto*, 1950), Luigi Comencini's *Bread, Love, and Dreams* and Dino Risi's *Poor But Beautiful* (*Poveri ma belli*, 1957), such films displayed neither the political commitment nor the artistic innovation of neorealism and what realism they had was reassuring rather than revealing. They were criticised in Italy by the PCI and in France by Bazin, but their popularity pointed to an appetite for easily digestible cinema which was central to the consolidation of the commercial Italian cinema as it grew both in output and in domestic and foreign revenue through the 1950s and into the 1960s.

Against these odds, however, neorealism remained a vital part of Italian and international film culture, at least until the mid-1950s, although it rarely again matched the combined commercial and critical success of *Rome, Open City* and *Bicycle Thieves*. The political battle for neorealism had two important effects: conservative interests managed to break the special relationship which briefly flourished between popular audiences and critical film culture; and political conformism impacted upon the formal and thematic procedures of neorealist filmmakers, forcing them to look for new aesthetic directions and even to monitor how they described their films in public.

The critical debate

One positive outcome of the ideological struggle surrounding neorealism was a rich film critical discourse, to which filmmakers themselves contributed. As Francesco Casetti has observed, the era saw the 'widespread acceptance of cinema as a cultural fact' (1999: 8). Neorealism inspired intense debate on the nature and meaning of the cinematic medium itself, most of it driven by a belief in cinema as an enlightening, even utopian, cultural form. This was an exciting moment which would influence later Italian filmmakers such as Pasolini, Olmi and Rosi, and which would have a tremendous impact on the French, British and American 'new wave' cinemas of the 1960s and on the postcolonial cinemas of Brazil, India, Egypt and elsewhere. As Miriam Hansen has explained, the German film historian Siegfried Kracauer, one of the most important champions of cinematic realism in the post-war period, 'understood the cinema as an alternative public sphere – alternative to both bourgeois institutions of art, education and culture and the traditional arenas of politics – a discursive horizon through which, however compromised by its capitalist foundations, something like an actual democratisation of culture seemed to be taking place' (1997: xi). In Italy and in France where the critical discourse of realism was most developed, two key perspectives prevailed – humanist and Marxist, corresponding to left-liberal and leftist – although in practice large areas of overlap existed between the two.

Luigi Chiarini (1900–1975), the director of the Centro Sperimentale, and the founder and editor of *Bianco e nero* until 1951, had directed films including the calligraphist *Five Moons Street* but in later years became the best known of the Italian humanist critics. Stressing the variety of styles which co-existed under the umbrella term neorealism, he defended it as 'a condemnation of certain social systems' which was much more valuable than 'cinematic spectacle', but cautioned that neorealist films deteriorated in quality the more explicitly they articulated 'the programme of a political party' (1979: 141). Umberto Barbaro was a colleague of Chiarini's at the Centro Sperimentale where he was an influential professor, contributor to *Bianco e nero*, and translator of Russian film theory. After the war, he co-scripted De Santis's *The Tragic Hunt* and taught in Poland before becoming chief film critic at *L'Unità*. Like most Marxists, he believed that the Crocean tradition of idealist aesthetics had been implicated in the rise of fascism and saw neorealism as a counter-tendency deeply-rooted in Italian popular tradition. Inspired by the model of Soviet cinema, he saw film as a social and political intervention, the artist as an activist. He was skeptical of the objectivist documentary ideal of neorealism proposed by Zavattini and even criticised Visconti's *Ossessione* and *La terra trema* for political vagueness. In the 1950s, he moved closer to a socialist realist position which led him to some unfortunately hardline condemnations of the experiments with neorealism by Rossellini, Antonioni and Fellini.

The film criticism of Guido Aristarco was also Marxist but more subtle. Aristarco was a contributor to *Cinema* in the early 1940s, its editor from 1949 to 1952, and founder-editor of its descendant *Cinema nuovo*. His only work in cinema was in co-scripting *Il sole sorge ancora* but, as a professor at the University of Milan, he published influential books including *L'Arte del film* (1950) and *Storia delle teoriche del film* (1951). Aristarco was the most important proponent of the 'historical-materialist' realism advocated by the Hungarian literary theorist, Georg Lukács, who argued that the nineteenth-century historical novels of such authors as Tolstoy and Balzac offered the best model for revolutionary literature in the twentieth century. Aristarco argued that, rather than rely on the simple interaction of camera and environment, realist cinema should rely on the creative intervention of the filmmaker applied to adaptations of historical novels whose detailed reconstructions of the past could enlighten viewers on the possibility of a better collective future. This led Aristarco to praise Visconti's *La terra trema* and *Senso* for marking steps from 'neorealism' to 'realism', although Aristarco also warned against purist, authoritarian versions of socialist realism and was prepared to accept the experiments of Fellini and Antonioni in the 1950s with 'imagination, dream and invention' (1955a: 111).

In France, André Bazin enthusiastically welcomed the new directions which neorealism took in the 1950s, although his politics were not leftist but aligned with a distinctive anti-Establishment Catholic humanism which flourished in France after the war. Writing in the journals *Esprit* and *Cahiers du cinéma*, Bazin was one of the most influential critics to promote the idea of neorealism as a revolutionary school of cinema both in form and content. Strongly conditioned by the French experience of war, occupation and collaboration with fascism, and very conscious of the philosophical ramifications of the Nazi Holocaust and the Cold War, Bazin's film criticism was idealistic in its ethics, with parallels to the Existentialism of Sartre, Camus and Merleau-Ponty, for whom life was a series of absolute moral choices. It was on this level that *Bicycle Thieves* was particularly resonant for Bazin, although he acknowledged that the film was also a critique of modern urban society and dehumanising capitalism. Bazin argued that the post-war world was in need of spiritual renewal, a belief which often put him at odds with the materialism of Marxist critics whom he accused of sometimes elevating 'social reality to a transcendental state' (1971a: 73). Nevertheless, Bazin held that neorealists could be 'materialists, Christians, Communists, or whatever' (1971a: 99). Calling for cinema to observe a 'straightforward cinematographic respect for the unity of space', he was sympathetic to the neorealism of Zavattini, although reckoning that Zavattini's plan for a cinema of 'ninety minutes in the life of a man to whom nothing happens' was 'an unrealisable project' (1985: 180). His most important consideration was not that a film be absolute in its adherence to a neorealist ideal but that it maintain a neorealist frame, even if that included moments of contrived *mise-en-scène* and classical editing as had *Bicycle Thieves*.

Zavattini was also a humanist with leftist sympathies. After fascism, war and liberation, he argued that 'the space between life and spectacle must disappear' (1979: 103) in cinema, turning his back on much of his work in commercial cinema of the 1930s to become one of the most important neorealist practitioners and one of its most important advocates in writings and public interventions. Zavattini criticised commercial cinema for what he saw as its destruction of art and truth, arguing that 'when a director evades the analysis of "everyday occurrences" he obeys the more or less expressed desires of the capitalistic system of cinema production' (1979: 74). His sympathies focused on the poor, the elderly and children, all marginalised figures in post-war Italian society. He shared a belief in cinema as truth with Bazin and Kracauer and with filmmakers such as Dziga Vertov and John Grierson, although his position was arguably the most purely documentarist of all, relying on 'an unlimited confidence in things, events, and in men' (1979: 68).

Zavattini aimed for an almost completely un-mediated representation of reality by the camera, accepting only the most elementary technical intervention by director and crew in the preparation and filming of a subject and in post-production. He proposed a realism much purer than that achieved in most of his films with De Sica, with the exception of certain sequences of *Umberto D*. The producer Carlo Ponti offered him a chance to direct his own feature film, but Zavattini never did. The composite film *Love in the City* (*Amore in città*, 1953) which he conceived, and for which he co-directed one episode with Francesco Maselli, was intended to be an actuality film which would bring together a range of neorealist styles (the other episodes were by Risi, Fellini, Lattuada, Lizzani and Antonioni). Zavattini's episode, 'Storia di Caterina' was a reconstruction of the real-life of a young woman forced by poverty to give up her child. But Zavattini himself acknowledged that the episode, and the film as a whole, was imperfectly achieved and *Love in the City* was seized upon by Zavattini's critics as evidence of the failure of his view of neorealism as pure documentation. Nonetheless, Zavattini's achievement as a writer and thinker was radical and inspiring. During a visit to Budapest in 1956, he argued against socialist realism on the grounds that all art is socialist to begin with:

> What is socialist realism except this awareness of the artist's constant responsibility toward life, political life? ... Art is socialist ... it can only be socialist. Even when the artist doesn't want it to be ... The great new fact of the post-war period – and it was also felt in Italian neorealism – was the socialist artist's humble and enthusiastic acceptance of a fighting role... (1970: 105–6)

De Sica in the early 1950s

Zavattini and De Sica followed *Bicycle Thieves* with *Miracle in Milan*, *Umberto D* and *The Gold of Naples*, each of which tried to expand neorealism, but with varying degrees of success. *Miracle in Milan* portrayed the deprivation and displacement of a community of tramps and poor migrants on wasteland planned for development by real estate speculators. The film's imagery of rain-drenched streets and the paraphernalia of urban modernity, streetcars and advertisements, was presented through the naïve young protagonist, Toto. Satirically, De Sica contrasted the tramps' shanty town of cardboard and scrap timber huts with the sophisticated city centre of Milan in order to suggest, in line with *Shoeshine* and *Bicycle Thieves*, that there had been only superficial change in the fundamental social structure since the end of fascism. *Miracle in Milan* also used a mixture of professional and non-professional actors, but its neorealism was complicated by prominent elements of fantasy – for example, the magical ability of Toto's white dove to relieve poverty by creating material goods in the blink of an eye, and the final sequence of the film which shows the tramps escaping the city by literally flying away from it on broomsticks. Zavattini defended the film by arguing that its social message was most important: 'The fundamental emotion of *Miracle in Milan* is not one of escape (the flight at the end), but of indignation, a desire for solidarity with certain people, a refusal of it with others. The film's structure is intended to suggest that there is a great gathering of the humble ones against the others' (quoted in Armes, 1971: 166). But the film's fantastical elements interfered with its otherwise sound neorealist premise and content and the film was neither a critical nor commercial success.

Bazin tactfully rationalised *Miracle in Milan* as a 'parenthesis' between *Bicycle Thieves* and *Umberto D* (1985: 180). Only with difficulty did De Sica manage to persuade producer Angelo Rizzoli to finance the latter's small budget and De Sica regularly had difficulty raising production money despite the success of *Bicycle Thieves*. *Umberto D* stands as one of the most important examples of neorealist cinema and the closest to a realisation of Zavattini's project. In it, he and De Sica turn from a working-class to a middle-class subject, the lead character Umberto being a dignified elderly gentleman who lives in poverty in a Rome boarding house, unable to pay his rent and forced to beg. The fact that certain interior sequences were filmed at Cinecittà is outweighed by the affecting naturalistic performance of the role of Umberto by the non-professional actor Carlo Di Battisti, in real life a University of Florence professor. The film uses a sophisticated range of slow traveling shots, deep-focus filming, and long takes in order to emphasise Umberto's marginalisation in Roman society, a marginalisation underlined by strong contrasts between his humble apartment and the hostile city outside. These techniques also underpin the film's innovative description of physical reality in something approaching real time. Bazin praised its lack of classical narrative structure and its '"unimportant" actions ... recorded for us in strict temporal continuity' (1971a: 78), singling out the now-famous scene in which the camera studies every movement and object as the housemaid Maria wakes in morning and proceeds to make coffee in the kitchen. However, it was the political rather than artistic implications of the film which concerned Giulio Andreotti in his attack on the film which, coming just a few weeks after its release, must have had some role in its box-office failure.

De Sica and Zavattini's phase of neorealist creativity ended with *The Gold of Naples* which presented four simple portraits of everyday Neapolitan family life. The film appeared at first to lean towards *neorealismo rosa* in deploying touristic images of the Bay of Naples, street musicians and vendors, schoolchildren, shoppers, gallerias and cafés. However, its first two comic episodes, which had working-class settings and did tend towards quaintness, soon gave way to two darkly melodramatic episodes with bourgeois settings and characters which cleverly recast an idyllic Naples as a place of entrapment. *The Gold of Naples* was commercially unsuccessful, but the De Sica and Zavattini partnership had already begun to decline with the romance *Stazione Termini*, a star vehicle for the American actors Montgomery Clift and Jennifer Jones, which would be followed by the conventional comedies *Two Women* (*La ciociara*, 1960) and *Yesterday, Today and Tomorrow* (*Ieri, oggi, domani*, 1963), of which Zavattini, in particular, was not very proud in later years.

Visconti in the early 1950s

A different trajectory was followed by Luchino Visconti who successfully made the transition from neorealism to become one of the most important directors in Italy's explosion of art cinema in the 1960s and 70s. After *La terra trema*, his *Bellissima* centered on an obsessive mother, Maddalena Cecconi (Anna Magnani) who enters her daughter in a beauty contest at Cinecittà designed to find the most beautiful girl in Rome. As Geoffrey Nowell-Smith has put it, the film was intended as a critique of 'the cultural sickness of the contemporary Italian scene' (2003: 46). With a script by Zavattini, a working-class setting, and characters speaking the authentic dialect of *romanesco*, it carried neorealist hallmarks but its light-hearted comedy and melodrama set it somewhat apart from the rest of Visconti's generally political *oeuvre*.

However, *Senso*, Visconti's next film, returned firmly to politics, present-ing a complex narrative of the formation of Italy during the Risorgimento, set in Austrian-controlled Venice in 1866 and revolving around an Italian countess who is sympathetic to her nation's fight for independence but who falls in love with an Austrian officer. The film is constituted by a mean-ingful tension between a detailed social landscape of peasants and sol-diers filmed on location in Venice and its environs and an opulent *mise-en-scène* involving rich sets, period costumes and crowd scenes, all filmed in Technicolor. This allowed Visconti to comment on the decadence of Italy's nineteenth-century bourgeoisie but also, by implication, on what Visconti saw as the decadence of the bourgeois Christian Democrat Italy after World War Two. The film's doom-laden ending, in which the countess goes mad and the Austrian officer is executed, was far from Andreotti's prescription for 'a healthy and constructive optimism'. The Christian Democrat govern-ment, the army, and other conservative elements attacked it as a left-wing allegory which made the unacceptable suggestion that the Risorgimento was not a popular national struggle but a revolution of the middle class against the aristocracy from which the working class and peasants gained little. The film's producers, Lux, agreed to cuts without which it would not have been exhibited. At the same time, Visconti was criticised by Chiarini, Zavattini and others for what they saw as his corruption of neorealism – understandably, many people remained wary of lavish historical dramas because they had been so beloved of the fascists. However, *Senso* was strongly supported by Guido Aristarco for whom it was 'a revolutionary film that brought our cinematic history to a new peak' (1955b: 196). *Senso* was exactly the film Aristarco had been waiting for, answering his call for a historical-materialist realism akin to that of Lukács. He welcomed the film for moving beyond neorealism into 'critical realism'.

In the early 1950s, the anti-fascist resistance and post-war austerity which had inspired the emergence of neorealism had been transformed, as had the terms in which neorealist cinema was viewed, described and debated. Under siege from the Establishment and regurgitated in dilute form by the commercial film industry, neorealism would continue only as a 'neorealism on the defensive', as Alberto Farassino has put it, and the films of Rossellini, Visconti, Antonioni and Fellini would be 'oases in the desert' (1998: 78), a culture of opposition rather than of the mainstream. To many the new directions laid out by *Miracle in Milan*, *Umberto D*, *Senso* and *La Strada* marked a 'crisis of neorealism' which was not only artistic but betrayed unwelcome changes in Italian society and politics. Many overt leftists such as De Santis and Lizzani became marginalised, De Sica and Zavattini's neorealism went into decline, and Visconti moved toward historical melodrama. As we shall see in the next chapter, Antonioni's *Cronaca di un amore*, Rossellini's *Journey to Italy* and Fellini's *The Nights of Cabiria* took neorealism in the direction of metaphor and abstraction. Some, such as Chiarini and Bazin, welcomed these new directions because they enriched neorealism; others welcomed them because they broke with what Galvano della Volpe called Zavattini's 'banality of authenticity' (1972: 15). For others still, especially Marxist critics, these films marked a radical break with neorealism in their self-conscious visual style and philosophical introspection.

In December 1953, an important Congress on Neo-Realist Cinema was held in Parma, bringing together filmmakers, critics and the public to evaluate neorealism at what seemed a crucial turning point and in the face of ongoing attacks from government, the Catholic Church and other conservative interests. Rossellini continued to receive criticism for his allegedly pro-American and pro-Christian Democrat positions, but this was unfair. As he explained, the critical and commercial failure in 1947 of his *Germany Year*

Zero came amid the restoration of Hollywood and domestic commercial cinema in Italy and presented him with a crunch decision in which he felt forced to choose between 'prostitution or sincerity' (1979: 100). Choosing the latter, he became increasingly experimental in *Stromboli*, *The Machine to Kill Bad People*, *Europa '51* and *Journey to Italy*. Fellini, whose *La Strada* was praised by Bazin but lambasted by Aristarco, criticised all restrictive views of neorealism, quipping, 'Why should people go to the movies if films show reality only through a very cold and objective eye? It would be better just to walk around in the street' (quoted in Armes 1971: 195). His films of the 1950s introduced new degrees of fantasy verging on magical realism, but he saw them as neorealist in so far as neorealism was for him 'a way of seeing reality without prejudice' (quoted in Armes 1971: 199). The concept of neorealism expanded significantly beyond the simple visual reproduction of reality but notions of a break with neorealism were tremendously exaggerated.

Some films which expanded upon neorealism, such as *Cronaca di un amore*, shifted attention from working-class to middle-class subjects but others such as *The Nights of Cabiria* did not, and in any case the concern with middle-class subjects did not in itself end neorealism but broadened its examination of class in general. Many films such as *Journey to Italy* became more interested in psychological than material hardship, but others such as *The Nights of Cabiria* merged the two seamlessly. All of these films remained firmly engaged with location filming, using exterior reality not only to comment on material deprivation but, metaphorically, on psychological alienation too. Antonioni, Rossellini and Fellini all moved towards greater and greater narrative and visual complexity – relying on aimless characters, dissolved linear narratives, abstract cinematography and absences of narrative closure – but all of these had already been evident in De Sica's *Bicycle Thieves*. As the next chapter shall explain, these developments fulfilled rather than contradicted the internal logic of neorealism and lend weight to a view of neorealism as a phenomenon which continued well into the 1950s.

5   NEOREALISM'S SECOND PHASE

Cronaca di un amore

Michelangelo Antonioni came from a middle-class background in Ferrara and was educated at the University of Bologna before becoming a film critic for the Ferrara newspaper *Corriere Padano* in 1935 and then, moving to Rome, for the journal *Cinema* in 1939. In 1940 his reviews of the Venice Film Festival, of which Mussolini was a great supporter, revealed his disillusion with the commercialism and superficiality of the mainstream film industry (1940a and 1940b). Antonioni studied at the Centro Sperimentale, scripted Rossellini's *Un pilota ritorna* in 1941, and assisted Marcel Carné in the production of his *Les visiteurs du soir* in Paris in 1942. The following year, he praised Visconti's *Ossessione* in his review of the film, and especially its detailed realist portrayal of everyday Italian life and the rural landscape. At this time Antonioni began to direct his own films. He shot the documentary *Gente del Po* (1943) with the support of the Istituto LUCE in the Po valley, focusing on the everyday activities and habitats of field labourers, boat workers and families, whom he showed living in close harmony with the river and its surrounding lands. Indeed, in the decades since, Antonioni has claimed that, if the original negative of *Gente del Po* had not been stolen by the fascists soon after filming and left to rot in a warehouse, his own early discovery of neorealism might have been more widely recognised (1996: 194). Antonioni's next film, also a documentary, followed this rural representation with a focus on Rome. *Nettezza Urbana* (1948) was filmed in what would become Antonioni's distinctive style – a slow and controlled moving camera, remaining at a distance from its human subject by favouring medium and long shots over close-ups. Here, to the accompaniment of a minimal soundtrack consisting of little explanatory voice-over but mostly jazz and Bach, Antonioni presented the activities of sanitation workers in famous parts of the city such as the Piazza del Popolo and Piazza del Quirinale, but in the early morning while they were still deserted.

Both films demonstrated a sensitivity to the hardships faced in daily life by ordinary Italians which would remain central throughout Antonioni's career. In this respect, Antonioni's early filmmaking can be described as 'neorealist', a credential supported by his contribution to the script of De Santis's *The Tragic Hunt*. Antonioni's visual style was neorealist in the priority it gave to observation as a virtue in itself, as a means of social documentation, and as a rejection of the commercialising and glamorising tendencies of mainstream cinema, whether Italian or from Hollywood. That is not to say that Antonioni wore his political views on his sleeve – he was never a strong leftist as were many neorealists, and he usually steered clear of party political involvement with the exception of his brief work for the republican Action Party during the anti-fascist resistance from 1943 to 1945. Partly as a result of his experience of fascism, but also because of his wariness of the rigid ideological lines along which both the Right and Left became defined during the Cold War, Antonioni generally sought to evade didactic interpretations of his films. His sensitivity to social hardship occasionally led to difficulties – for example, *I vinti* (1953) controversially represented problems of modern family life, including juvenile delinquency, and fell victim to heavy cutting by the censors – but in general Antonioni sought to communicate political and social meaning in his films in relatively abstract ways.

His first feature film, *Cronaca di un amore*, was made in 1950 when the immediate difficulties of post-war destruction and austerity were beginning to lift and in a style which demonstrated Antonioni's relationship to Italian neorealism to be one of questioning and yet positive adaptation. In an atmosphere of increasing material comfort, Antonioni felt it appropriate to expand the neorealist focus on the working class by representing people from his own middle-class background. In *Cronaca di un amore*, Antonioni focused on the anguish of a settled but dissatisfied young woman, Paola, whose empty and unfulfilling marriage to a rich industrialist, Enrico Fontana, leads her to rejuvenate a destructive romance and sexual liaison with a former lover, Guido, despite the fact that his drifter-lifestyle cannot provide her with the material luxuries to which she is accustomed. For Antonioni, the middle-class focus was in keeping with the changing character of Italian society, economics and politics – and the changing character of Italian cinema – as the country recovered slowly from the war. In *Cronaca di un amore*, Antonioni probes the emptiness of bourgeois society to question the terms upon which Italy's recovery was founded. His middle-class focus was seen by many as a betrayal of neorealist principles, but it in fact strengthened the key neorealist concern with class by turning the camera on the bourgeoisie who were the bedrock upon which the new dominance of the Christian Democrats and liberal capitalism were founded.

At the same time, Antonioni, like Rossellini and Fellini in the 1950s, extended neorealism's concern with the visible world into a preoccupation with the subjective difficulties of mental alienation, although the exterior documentation of material conditions remained important. His focus on what Peter Brunette calls 'the not-seen' (1998: 18) did not represent an end of neorealism in Antonioni's work, as Brunette suggests. Even in *Rome, Open City*, *Paisà* and *Germany Year Zero*, Rossellini had been profoundly concerned with non-visible issues such as the unrepresentable horror of torture, the indignity of military occupation, the nobility of self-sacrifice in war, the difficulty of moral reconstruction after it – and De Sica's *Bicycle Thieves* was not only about the theft of a bicycle but the crisis of self-esteem and self-identity which that theft occasioned in one man and which indicated the crisis of an entire people at a unique moment in their history. For Antonioni, all of his work from *Gente del Po* and *Netteza Urbana*, to *Cronaca di un amore*, *I vinti* and even *Il grido*, was firmly neorealist. It differed from the late 1940s films of Rossellini, Visconti, De Sica, De Santis and others not in not being neorealist but in the terms of its neorealism which Antonioni liked to describe as 'interior neorealism' (1996: 159).

In its narrative of sexual intrigue leading to a conspiracy to murder, *Cronaca di un amore* was indebted to American *film noir* and to Visconti's *Ossessione* – indeed, the male lead in both films was Massimo Girotti. But *Cronaca di un amore* was only superficially generic. Antonioni pointed out that the word 'cronaca' in the film's title was intended to mean 'chronicle' in the sense of the documentation of exterior reality associated with Rossellini in *Paisà*. Antonioni sought a narrative structure which would not present a clear and controlled exposition of logically-organised events as in classical cinema but a series of actions and pieces of information only loosely organised and barely explained as if captured from real life with a minimum of directorial intervention or commentary. The narrative structure of *Cronaca di un amore* is only tenuously linear and the viewer's ability to follow it is constantly challenged by Antonioni's refusal to fully explain his characters' origins, motivations and actions.

Fig. 10 Guido and Paola on the outskirts of Milan in *Cronaca di un amore*

This is clear in the film's enigmatic opening which throws us straight into the action with no initial exposition as we are presented with an office in which a discussion is in progress between private investigators who are working on some sort of case which seems to pertain to a young woman whose background her husband wishes to know more about for reasons which are not stated. The main characters are introduced to us at second hand as a detective traces the personal history of Paola at her old school in Ferrara, building witnesses' accounts into a picture of an intelligent and well-liked, though restless, young woman. In due course, we see Guido visit Milan to inform a worried Paola that a detective has been asking questions about her past but Antonioni is slow to explain their relationship and it is only eventually, after three different encounters – outside a theatre, beside a rugby pitch on the outskirts of the city, in a car driving back roads to avoid being spotted – that we understand that Paola and Guido were once lovers, that they were involved in some sort of deadly accident, and that Paola is now desperately unhappy in marriage and wants to get out. Indeed, it is only subsequently that we understand the kind of accident Paola and Guido were mixed up in – the private investigator reads an old newspaper headline from 1943 which reports the death of a young woman after a fatal fall down an elevator shaft in a building on the via Verdi. Antonioni delays the pace and complicates the order in which necessary pieces of narrative information are released to the viewer, interfering with the processes of viewing associated with classical narrative. This strategy peaks in the climax to the film in which Guido waits by a bridge in the night intending to ambush and kill Paola's husband, Enrico, on his way home from work, while Paola prepares to entertain guests at home. We see Enrico read the report on his wife's background submitted to him by the detectives, then set off for home, agitated, while Paola waits for a phone call from Guido to tell her the murder is committed, and Guido waits in the shadows for Enrico's car to approach. Suddenly, however, just as we expect a dramatic encounter, we hear in the distance a car, what sound like two gunshots, and some dogs barking. With Guido, we wonder what has happened, gradually following him as he cycles some distance to what turns out to be a burning car – indeed, we realise, the wreck of Enrico's car, smashed into a ditch, apparently by careless driving. The dramatic encounter never happens, we never know what Enrico was thinking just before he died, why his vehicle spun off the road, or what he intended to do when he arrived home to Paola. When the police arrive at Paola's home to tell her of her husband's death, she panics, thinking they have come to arrest her. Guido explains it was all an accident but we are denied the happy ending of their romantic union which a genre film would deliver as Antonioni instead presents a bewilderingly disjointed dialogue:

> *Guido*: Now we can't go on anymore.
> *Paola*: Why not?
> *Guido*: Don't you feel it?

He promises to phone the next day, leaving her in stony silence in the doorway as he sets off for the train station in the rain. The film ends, refusing any moral judgment of its protagonists' actions and leaving behind a chasm of uncertainty not only as to Guido's decision to abandon Paola just when it would seem that a bizarre accident has freed them to be together, but also as to their role in the original elevator accident in 1943 which brought them together in the first place. Thus Antonioni presents us with something resembling a *film noir* but recounted in the disjointed and unreliable manner first demonstrated by Rossellini in the Florence sequence of *Paisà* in which, as the nurse Harriet negotiates the difficult terrain of a bombed-out city in search of her lover, the fog of war makes a comprehensive and authoritative understanding of events impossible and information arrives sporadically and incomplete.

Indeed, in *Cronaca di un amore*, this realism of event and information is accompanied by a distinctive realism of visual form. Antonioni's sophisticated cinematography consists primarily of long and medium shots filmed with a slowly moving camera in long takes which emphasise the alienation of the human subject by his or her physical environment. This somewhat detached mode of photographic observation is deployed to striking effect in interior sequences. In the first scene, the camera rotates enigmatically around the office in which the detectives discuss Paola's case; in Paola's home, the camera pans restlessly left and right as she weeps desperately on her bed. In one notable countryside sequence, where Paola and Guido meet on the bridge where they plan to murder Enrico, Antonioni's camera presents their nervous plotting and bickering in one continuous 360° panning shot, the quiet of the surrounding fields and riverbed disturbed by just one passing car and some distant workers. Many of Antonioni's shots are distinguished by their length and his avoidance of unnecessary editing in favour of the long take which provides a visual means of emphasising the forms, surfaces and textures of the physical habitat and its effects upon his characters' internal psychology. This style is at its most powerful when it engages in exterior sequences with the landscape of the city of Milan which Antonioni uses not only to comment on the city itself but also as a means of characterisation to suggest subjective emotional disposition within it. *Cronaca di un amore*, though Antonioni's first feature, already places the urban landscape to the fore. Often highlighting Milan's austere rationalist architecture (for example, Gio Ponti's landmark Montecatini Building, 1938), he develops the motif of the empty, lonely street which will become one of his hallmarks in *La signora senza camelie*, *I vinti* and *Il grido*. Antonioni also avoids close-ups and the melodramatic identification with character which they often encourage while downplaying the stardom of his performers in favour of an emphasis on the actor as another element of *mise-en-scène*. Antonioni's Milan is a rainy, dreary, industrial one in which we see occasional signs of social activity such as streetcars and traffic but which is predominantly characterised by an unnerving emptiness and anonymity and a lack of social energy and human warmth, especially in the depopulated marginal spaces where Guido and Paola secretly meet. This lack of energy and warmth is articulated in frequent shots of Paola and Guido as isolated individuals rather than as a couple and is matched by an absence of the social solidarity and ethics which characterised *Rome, Open*

Fig. 11 The empty, lonely street in *Cronaca di un amore*

City and *Bicycle Thieves*. These absences underpin Paola's alienation in the city and point to the increasingly privatised character of social organisation as the communal cohesion and ethical responsibility of the immediate post-war era give way to the individualism and consumerism of a resurgent capitalist economy.

Although in *Cronaca di un amore* the problem of material poverty does not present itself, therefore, the problem of spiritual poverty is no less critical. It is not an immediate social crisis but a creeping private one. If the city is hostile, the private world of the home offers little compensation. Paola's domestic environment is a pampered, bourgeois one comprising luxury apartments and boutiques, her dissatisfaction only barely masked by richly decorated interiors, the good manners of society ladies and mean-ingless discussions about the latest fashion styles. Beyond it, she officially ventures only for evenings among the idle rich at La Scala, where Guido first spots her dressed in white fur. Like many of the female protagonists which Antonioni became famous for in later films, Paola is acutely aware of her alienation, recognising her status as just another commodity for her husband, Enrico, of no greater importance than his purchase of a sports car on a whim: 'He loves no-one, buys everything. He bought me.' Enrico, meanwhile, seems more at home and competent in the white-collar work environment of the boardroom, surrounded by typewriters, intercoms and the technological paraphernalia of office life, than he does in his private relations with her. Their relationship is not one of trust but one of spying, mediated by the figure of the detective whose constant shadowing of Paola exacerbates her experience of the city as a hostile space.

But the alienation which haunts Paola and Guido is not only that of the present of modern urban Italy – it is also a haunting of that present by a dark secret from the recent past. The young woman killed in the elevator shaft in 1943 was not an anonymous victim but Guido's then-girlfriend, Giovanna, and her death cleared the way for Guido and Paola to become involved. Paola does her best to reassure herself and Guido that although Giovanna used to be 'between' them, 'We didn't do anything and we're free. You're mine. You're here. We didn't save her, and now we can have each other.' Her words acknowledge some responsibility for Giovanna's death (though how responsible they were is never clear), and a morbid guilt seems to haunt Guido throughout the film. However, their continuing arguments about the past soon suggest that even with Enrico dead they are unlikely to find happiness. In the film's final moments, as the camera lingers on Paola standing bereft in a shadowy doorway, we can only speculate as to what she, or Guido, must be thinking. Thus Antonioni is preoccupied with the question of the relevance of the past in a manner which echoes *Paisà*, *Germany Year Zero* and *Umberto D*. In *Cronaca di un amore*, the year 1943 witnessed the death of Giovanna but, in Italian history, it witnessed the fall of Italian fascism, the death of the nation's dark secret with which it was still coming to terms in 1950. Arguably, *Cronaca di un amore* is also a chronicle of Italian history, an allegory of the transformation of a society and a rupture in human relationships forced by the emergence from a brutal past. However, Antonioni holds back from spelling out any such conclusion. Just as the film's narrative structure was constituted by gaps in the flow of information, its final scene remains enigmatically on 'the surface of the world' as Seymour Chatman has put it (1985: 3), presenting an expressionless Paola stranded on an expressionless street, both revealing nothing more than the suppression of human emotion by the surfaces of modern urban life.

It is unfortunate that so many accounts treat Antonioni's early films, including *Cronaca di un amore*, as little more than experiments by a filmmaker who would not come into his own until the 1960s with *L'avventura*, *L'eclisse* and *La notte*. Through these later films, Antonioni is rightly identified as one of the most important modernist filmmakers whose concerns with visual and thematic ambiguity and metaphysical alienation traveled beyond the original neorealist concern with the immediate social conditions of post-war Italy. Examination of *Cronaca di un amore*, however, reminds us of the rich phase of neorealism in which Antonioni was engaged in his early career. As late as 1958, indeed, although Antonioni argued that 'it no longer seems to me important to make a film about a man who has had his bicycle stolen', he was careful also to assert that neorealism was not 'over' but was 'evolving' (1996: 7–8). That evolution continued the neorealist questioning of Italy's post-war reconstruction not by concentrating on poverty, inequality or physical devastation but on what Antonioni suggested was a fundamental spiritual lack at the heart of capitalism which no abundance of material goods could ever address. Although his films did turn to the interior of characters, this turn did not signify a rejection of exterior reality but a desire to trace its effects beyond the problems of material austerity. This was a neorealism still very much concerned with the social but approaching its subject by subtly different means.

Journey to Italy

Roberto Rossellini's *Journey to Italy* comprises an expansion of neorealism in the direction of metaphysical or spiritual concerns and resembles the direction taken by Antonioni. Such concerns had always been present in Rossellini's neorealism but, after his so-called 'war trilogy' of *Rome, Open City*, *Paisà* and *Germany Year Zero*, they became more prominent in *Stromboli*, *Europa '51*, *Joan of Arc at the Stake* (*Giovanna d'Arco al rogo*, 1954) and *Journey to Italy*. These dealt with personal crises of alienation and despair although, unlike Antonioni, Rossellini was also interested in motifs of miraculous salvation. Throughout the 1950s, his examination of the human subject and human relationships in modernity displayed a greater religiosity of tone and frequently deployed Catholic iconography in a way which would never have occurred to Antonioni. On the other hand, both directors prioritised female perspectives in their films, and shared an interest in slowing down and opening up film narrative.

Rossellini's move was of particular significance given that he had epitomised, more than anyone else, the neorealist engagement with the horrors of war. In 1949, on the release of *Stromboli*, he declared 'you cannot go on shooting in ruined cities forever' (1985: 209). Although the themes of the everyday life and material hardships of ordinary Italians were never absent from his subsequent films, he became increasingly convinced that the most urgent issue facing the post-war world was not material but a great lack of vision, in the humanist or spiritual sense. This issue had been present in *Germany Year Zero* and in the monastery sequence of *Paisà* which provided a study of the cultural encounter between an enclosed order of Italian monks and a visiting group of American army chaplains.

As Italy returned to peacetime normality, Rossellini became more interested in detecting underlying weaknesses in the social and moral status quo. The boy protagonist of *Germany Year Zero* and the monks of *Paisà* occupied outsider positions with respect to their larger societies and the figure of the outsider became central to Rossellini's films in the 1950s. A member of society and yet removed from it by extremes of suffering or madness, the outsider afforded a privileged perspective upon society and, by implication, a more truthful perception of its problems. In the episode entitled 'The Miracle' in *L'Amore*, directed by Rossellini but written by Federico Fellini, Anna Magnani played a naïve but religiously devout young shepherdess who miraculously becomes pregnant by Saint Joseph only to be ostracised by her disbelieving local community for whom she is the village idiot. In *Francis, God's Jester*, Rossellini contemplated the pure simplicity of the life of St Francis and his monks as a metaphor of the individual's relationship with God and other human beings, and in the absence of the distractions and material excesses of modern society. In *Europa '51*, Rossellini studied the grief and developing insanity of a well-to-do woman whose comfort and stability are rocked by the suicide of her son. In *The Machine to Kill Bad People*, the photographer Celestino gained a special perspective on the immorality and pettiness of his fellow townspeople from behind the lens of his camera whose miraculous power gave him an ability to paralyse bad people simply by taking their picture.

The key film which announced Rossellini's evolution after his war trilogy was *Stromboli*, the first film he made with his then lover and future wife, Ingrid Bergman, who had been so impressed by *Rome, Open City* that she jeopardised her Hollywood career in order to live and work with Rossellini in Italy. *Stromboli* took its cue from the war in so far as its narrative began with the marriage of its protagonist, Karin, to an Italian soldier who promises to take her away from the refugee camp where she is stranded to a new life on the small volcanic island which is his home. The film was shot entirely on location, with a rough script and small crew, on the real island of Stromboli which at the time lacked basic modern conveniences such as the telephone and electricity and whose impoverished community had recently come close to destruction by the island's volcano. Rossellini used the emptiness of this pre-modern volcanic landscape as a metaphor of the spiritual desolation which Karin falls into when life on the island turns out to be far from her expectations. Innovative long sequence shots emphasise the oppression of Karin by her alien surroundings and her increasingly hostile husband, Antonio, as Rossellini continues the strategy begun in *Germany Year Zero* of using exterior description to reveal interior states of mind. The setting is pre-modern but allows comment on modernity: the barren expanses of the island's surface may be read as an inversion of the densely-built space of the modern city and as a further refinement of the image of the wartorn urban landscape.

The theme of urban modernity which fascinated Rossellini throughout the post-war period is also at the centre of his enigmatic and profoundly moving *Journey to Italy* in which the city in question is neither the capital, Rome, nor industrial Milan, but the distinctively romantic southern city of Naples. An English couple, Alex and Katherine Joyce, arrive by car having driven all the way from England to take possession of a country villa recently left by a deceased uncle, Homer. Their physical journey, however, occasions a traumatic existential journey as the couple's marriage is in deep crisis and the trip affords them an opportunity for reflection. The narrative consists of little real action but a series of loosely connected events and encounters which Katherine and Alex have with Naples and its people during the few days it takes for the legalities of Homer's will to be resolved. The striking looseness of the narrative is enhanced by the fact that the protagonists spend most of the film apart, thus dividing the narrative line in two. Both protagonists seem to be stuck in empty routines of tourism as Katherine visits the museums and sights of the city and its environs, while Alex parties on the island of Capri where his frustration with his marriage leads him to flirt with the idea of having an affair. This dissolving of narrative builds upon Rossellini's earlier films and reflects his decreasing interest in the craft of the well-made story, an aspect of cinema which was always of less interest to him than it was to De Sica or Visconti. Much of the dialogue of *Journey to Italy* was developed during shooting, aiding the naturalism of the many sequences of small talk and everyday banter, but proving tremendously frustrating for George Sanders, who played Alex, in so far as it contradicted everything his background in Hollywood cinema led him to expect of professional performance. The long sequences were filmed with slow-moving or stationary cameras to create an impression of stillness and impassivity which Rossellini reinforced with a minimum of editing, encouraging the viewer to allow his/her eye to wander within the framed image and beyond its immediate signification. Digression became a deliberate part of the film and its meaning, contributing not only to the sense of aimless time passed by its protagonists but also to Rossellini's examination of the relationship between forward movement in time (the protagonists' physical journey, linear narrative, human mortality) and backward movement in time (the images of ancient cultures and primaeval landscapes which comprise the film's representation of Naples and its surroundings). This relationship is a subject in the very first sequence of the film in which Rossellini counterpoints the monotonous drone of the engine of the Joyces' Bentley, and rapid driving shots of roadside advertising billboards and a railway, with signs of traditional rural culture, a horse and cart and a herd of cattle blocking the road.

The city of Naples itself, however, becomes the focal point for the consideration of the relationship between modernity and the past. Beginning with the opening credits, the film uses Neapolitan ballads accompanied by romantic acoustic guitar to suggest Naples as the home of an authentic folk culture. The cinematography of Enzo Serafin, who also shot Antonioni's *Cronaca di un amore*, exploits what Giuliana Bruno calls Naples' 'intrinsically filmic' qualities (1997: 46) to present the city, its bay, Mount Vesuvius, and the island of Capri, as places of sublime Mediterranean beauty, bathed in shimmering sunlight. These natural settings, combined with a rich ancient heritage and prosperous port, made the city an important stop on the European Grand Tour of the eighteenth and nineteenth centuries and continue to draw tourists to the smart hotels and sophisticated bars and restaurants which make up the modern Neapolitan tourist industry we see in the film.

Although Alex and Katherine arrive on family business, most modern visitors to Naples are attracted to it precisely because of its relatively pristine preservation of traditional architecture and ways of life which have long since vanished from other twentieth-century cities. As the capital of the *mezzogiorno*, and a city which has historically been disproportionately affected by poverty and industrial underdevelopment, Naples in *Journey to Italy* is neither an industrial-technological hub on the scale of Milan nor a centre of metropolitan culture and government like Rome. Rossellini focuses on its anachronistic character: its timeless natural vistas, including the museum of archaeology, the caves of the Sibyll at Cumae, the lava beds at Pozzuoli, the Fontanella catacombs and the nearby ruins of Pompeii. These signify Naples' peculiar resistance to urban modernity and its distinctively dispersed urban geography. As Victor Burgin has explained, this aspect of Naples fascinated Walter Benjamin who visited the city in 1924. Naples' distinctive 'porous' architecture of narrow lanes, busy piazzas, secret courtyards and passageways, in the constant presence of the sea, signified for Benjamin 'the survival of pre-capitalist social forms which had not yet succumbed to the modern segregation of life into public and private zones' (quoted in Burgin 1998: 59; see also Benjamin 1986). The sense of Naples as a city in which life is played out on the street was all too evident in Rossellini's depiction of displaced Neapolitan families living in caves in *Paisà*, but a different life in the streets is prominent in *Journey to Italy* in which several scenes show Katherine driving through the city, pleasantly struck by the energy of everyday life: men sitting in cafés, roadworkers, a funeral cortège, lovers in a park, mothers and babies, nuns, and a priest crossing the street in front of a row of 'Vote Communist' election posters. As André Bazin approvingly observed, these sequences are 'as objective as a straight photograph' and yet they are also elements in 'a mental landscape' (1971a: 98) identified with Katherine's subjective point of view and deriving their meaning from the striking contrast between their happy public activity and the private anguish she feels as her marriage falls apart.

However, the Joyces' marital crisis is really a mechanism which allows Rossellini to investigate the pressures faced by human relationships in the

Fig. 12 Life in the streets of Naples in *Journey to Italy*

modern world. Rossellini presents their discord as an import from an alien culture in which social relations are governed by a more rigid organisation of time and of public and private space. As Laura Mulvey has persuasively argued, the film revolves around an opposition of northern to southern Europe, Anglo-Saxon to Latin culture (2000: 97). Alex's complaints about the excess of oil and garlic in Italian food, for example, reproduce clear national stereotypes. However, Alex and Katherine also come from a specific city – London – the epitome of northern European urban-industrial modernity. Their disagreeable bickering in the car makes clear that their relationship has been in difficulty for some time and, continuing throughout the film, its aggressive staccato seems more homologous with the white noise of downtown traffic than it does with the wind and waves of the Bay of Naples. While they jealously watch each other in public, at parties or dinner among friends, they book two rooms at their hotel and sleep in separate beds. In full-sleeved shirt, jacket and tie throughout the film, Alex is dressed more for the office than the Mediterranean sun and complains bitterly that the local culture 'poisons you with laziness'. More than once claiming to find Naples boring, he threatens to fly home alone. Katherine complains about the 'complete lack of modesty' of a museum-full of erotically-charged classical nudes where the elderly guide invites her to admire the attractive form of a female marble torso, and she leaves the caves of the Sibyll at Cumae in disgust after another guide pretends to tie her to the wall as if she was a female prisoner of the lustful Saracens. If Rossellini's Neapolitans are relaxed, sensual and earthy – squabbling young lovers, pregnant women, feisty old ladies and lascivious tour guides – Katherine and Alex suffer from an urban edginess and sexual repression which hampers their ability to enjoy the breezy eroticism with which the locals are so comfortable. Naples brings their crisis to a head, dropping them uncomfortably into an almost pastoral mode of leisure and reflection which only a city like Naples can indulge. Their misery is a function of their mutual estrangement but their time in Naples reveals that this estrangement is a function of a far deeper and shared alienation from the natural and human rhythms which are that city's special gift.

For Rossellini, discussing *Journey to Italy* in 1954, Naples was a symbol of 'the sense of eternal life' which modern urban societies tend to suppress but which is in need of rediscovery (1985: 211). Throughout most of the film, Alex and Katherine are in deep denial of their need for the existential therapy which Naples represents and it is only at the end of the film, when they embrace in a moment of miraculous reunification, that their encounters with it may be retrospectively re-read as a process of providential self-discovery and reconciliation. Although Alex storms off to the island of Capri hoping to prove his prowess with other women, his would-be romance with Marie comes to nothing and, returning to Naples, a late-night drive with a prostitute leaves him cold. Katherine, on the other hand, engages more actively with the city. The sculptures at the museum and the caves of the Sibyll bring her face to face with the ancient past but her impatience with the impenetrability of their stone surfaces and her prudish embarrassment at their eroticism initially blind her to the moving lessons they offer on the transience of human life. At the lava beds in Pozzuoli, like Karin in *Stromboli*, she must confront the timeless permanence of the living earth as the mysterious mechanics of the volcano allow her breath to produce its smoke, connecting her body to geological deep time. At the Fontanella catacombs – in reality a place of repose for the skeletons of paupers displaced from Naples' graveyards by nineteenth-century building – she is struck by the bizarre juxtaposition between macabre rows of skulls and her friend's earnest prayer for a baby.

Each of these 'metaphors of interconnectedness', as Angelo Restivo calls them (2002: 97), brings Katherine closer to the historical past and to nature, but it is her final encounter – with Pompeii – which is decisive. This time she is with Alex and they encounter the past and its meaning together. They watch the recovery of a cast of two victims of Vesuvius, a man and woman wrapped together at the moment of death, presumably in pain but also in an intimate embrace like lovers. Confronted by this humbling index of human mortality and communication, Katherine and Alex experience a moment of connection for the first time in the film as she breaks down and he runs after her with genuine concern, calling her by name. On a personal level, the image of the dead signifies the fragility of the human body and its need for completion by another. On a social level, however, it signifies the fragility of the city – the destruction of a great ancient Roman port by the overwhelming force of a volcano, in whose shadow the modern Naples continues to exist. *Journey to Italy* thus continues the figuration of the obliteration of the city which was directly depicted in the bombed Berlin of *Germany Year Zero* and obliquely in the primaeval volcanic landscapes of *Stromboli*. Rossellini's motifs of the pre-modern and of nature replay the destruction of human settlement by the overwhelming force of modern war and the victims of Vesuvius recall those of Dresden and Hiroshima.

In this light, the reconciliation of Alex and Katherine in a loving embrace in the final moments of the film seems not incongruous, as many critics of

Fig. 13 The fragility of the city; Pompeii in *Journey to Italy*

the film have complained, but logical and necessary. Driving back to the villa from Pompeii, Alex and Katherine are forced to stop their car by the sheer volume of crowds who have gathered to celebrate the religious festival of San Gennaro. They continue to argue and seem resolved to divorce. However, the movement of the crowds first sweeps them apart and then back together just as a statue of the Madonna passes in the procession and the crowd kneels in devotion. Their ultimate reunion, which, as André Bazin observed, epitomises the neorealist concern with 'pure acts' (1971a: 101), was in the offing among the ruins of Pompeii but comes to fruition as part of a collective act among the real people of modern Naples. Rossellini hones in on interior investigation and metaphysical questions but within a neorealist pattern in which outward documentation continues to play a central role and in which neorealist themes (World War Two), characters (the prostitute as signifier of poverty and moral crisis) and forms (documentary-style footage of everyday life) are indispensable. The final shot of *Journey to Italy* confirms the film's neorealist pedigree, withdrawing the camera from Katherine and Alex to the real faces of local people passing in the crowd.

Unfortunately, but perhaps understandably given the polarised political climate in which all debate on cinema took place in the mid-1950s, *Journey to Italy* was not a commercial success and was received with hostility by most critics both in Italy and abroad. Since *Stromboli*, Rossellini had never been able to recapture the combination of commercial success and critical acclaim which had greeted his first postwar films. His public image was further damaged by the sustained attacks he attracted from conservative Italians and, in one of neorealism's most important foreign markets, from conservative Americans: on both sides of the Atlantic outrage greeted certain supposedly blasphemous work, such as 'The Miracle', as well as his adulterous relationship with Ingrid Bergman whom many continued to resent for her desertion of Hollywood cinema. On the other hand, the film was also received with hostility by critics on the Italian left such as Guido Aristarco for whom, as explained in chapter four, Rossellini's turn to supposedly abstract humanist-philosophical concerns marked an unwelcome break with neorealism. The hostility of the right and left in Italy guaranteed the film's critical and commercial failure but it was received in France as an artistic milestone by André Bazin and the younger critics of *Cahiers du cinéma*.

Rossellini, who was consistently the most important neorealist for the *Cahiers* critics and for the French *nouvelle vague* of the 1960s, provided an ethically and visually inspiring cinema which was not available in contemporary France or from Hollywood. Jacques Rivette interpreted *Journey to Italy* as a metaphysical essay which achieved a thoroughly modern and perceptive portrayal of 'the *honnête homme* of 1953' (1985: 193). However, both he and his colleague and fellow future filmmaker Eric Rohmer interpreted the film in terms of their liberal Catholic faith, which they presumed Rossellini also shared but which was in fact different from his largely secular humanism. Rohmer's claim that God was an invisible third character in the film demonstrated the risks which filmmakers like Rossellini ran in the 1950s in trying to move neorealism any distance beyond social and material documentation. But a middle road was achieved by Bazin whose positive response to the film refused to limit neorealism to the documentary function alone while avoiding the theism of Rivette and Rohmer. In an open letter to Guido Aristarco, published in *Cinema nuovo* in 1955, Bazin agreed with the Marxist critic that commercial rip-offs of neorealism such as *Bread, Love, and Dreams* were unwelcome but he argued for a definition of neorealism not in terms of a specific social and political content but as 'a particular way of regarding things' (1971a: 97). The relativism implicit in a description of neorealism as a way of seeing rather than as a partisan cinema of the working class would continue to pose problems for critics on the left in years to come.

The Nights of Cabiria

Perhaps more than any other filmmaker, Federico Fellini pushed the boundaries of neorealism to their breaking point. From the provincial seaside
town of Rimini, Fellini moved to Rome in 1939 to begin his university education before working as a journalist, cartoonist and writer of short radio
dramas. His entrance to cinema was followed by his marriage to the student
actress Giulietta Masina, who would play leading roles in many of his films,
and his friendship with the comic actor Aldo Fabrizi, who played Don Pietro
in *Rome, Open City*. Through these connections, Fellini began screenwriting
film comedies and a close collaboration with the older Roberto Rossellini
which would see him contribute to *Rome Open City*, *Paisà*, 'The Miracle'
episode of *L'Amore*, and *Francis, God's Jester*, as well as Pietro Germi's
In the Name of the Law and Alberto Lattuada's *Without Pity*. Although, in
the 1960s, Fellini would become the most critically acclaimed and commercially successful of those directors who broke with neorealism, in the
decade after the end of the war he established a strong pedigree in the
aesthetics and ethics of neorealism which would inform his entire career.

Like Antonioni and Rossellini, Fellini recognised the special circumstances which gave rise to neorealism, declaring that 'After the war, the
subjects were ready-made. They were problems of a very simple kind:
survival, war, peace' (quoted in Leprohon 1972: 98). However, he always
viewed the notion of neorealism with an instinctive scepticism, and
insisted upon thinking of it not as a matter of social documentation alone
but as 'a way of seeing reality without prejudice, without conventions
coming between it and myself – facing it without preconceptions, looking
at it in an honest way – whatever reality is, not just social reality but all
that there is within a man' (quoted in Bondanella 2001: 32). The six films
he directed in the 1950s – *Variety Lights*, *The White Sheik*, *I vitelloni*, *La
Strada*, *Il bidone* and *The Nights of Cabiria* – employed realism as a window
on to internal character although, like the films of Antonioni and Rossellini,
they never strayed far from social concerns and presented their personal
tragedies as narratives with real social implications.

However, more than his peers, Fellini was convinced that directing a
film must involve a creative intervention into and shaping of reality, not
simply its reflection. Fellini's neorealism was thus a counter-tendency to
Zavattini's. This was clear in Fellini's interest in non-naturalistic performance achieved by heavy coaching of actors during filming. He never used
non-professionals in leading roles and, as a devotee of popular cultures

of illusion such as *la rivista*, comics and opera, many of the roles he drew from actors such as Giulietta Masina relied upon an explicit acknowledgment of the face of the performer as a mask. All of his films mixed neorealism with elements of comedy or farce which required actors to make frequent sudden changes in expression, mood or tone, contradicting the pure realism of performance other neorealists found in actors from the street. *Variety Lights*, which Fellini co-directed with Lattuada, announced Fellini's interest in the fragility of illusionism in its account of the mundane but sometimes magical life of a variety theatre company touring a series of seemingly-deserted provincial towns and cities. *The White Sheik*, based on a script originally drafted by Antonioni, examined the tension between reality and illusion by presenting two clashing responses to the city as it is experienced by a newlywed couple on honeymoon: the husband attracted to the real Rome of buildings, people and history, the wife to the Rome of high fashion and the glitzy fairytale photo stories known as *fotoromanzi*. The film's questioning of realist illusion was reinforced by a disruptive editing style and a disjointed musical soundtrack. This questioning was continued in *I vitelloni* where Fellini used subjective points of view and a nervously moving camera to suggest the tension and distraction of his bored and alienated young protagonists, stranded in the dull seaside town of Rimini, as each of them comes to a moment of disillusionment in which the mundane realities of life assert themselves over adolescent fantasies of fame, fortune and romance.

Fellini's *La Strada*, however, was the first film to achieve international success for his bittersweet and self-conscious brand of neorealism, winning the Academy Award for Best Foreign Picture in 1957. Like *Journey to Italy*, its narrative took the form of a journey by road which occasioned an existential journey for its protagonists, the bullying circus strongman Zampanò and his meek young female assistant Gelsomina. What he sees as her ugliness and stupidity prompt his macho contempt, her misery and their eventual separation, only to be followed by news of her unexplained death which leads him to an epiphany of grief and remorse and a recognition of the love for her which he suppressed. The film's reconfiguration of traditional, not to say Christian, ideas of suffering and redemption, at the heart of what was a neorealist film in its visual observation of rural life and in its open-ended narrative, made it one of the most telling signs of the so-called 'crisis of neorealism' and attracted the censure of Guido Aristarco who objected to its 'poetry of the solitary man' (quoted in Bondanella 2001: 134). Fellini, however, was quick to respond, arguing that 'There are more Zampanòs in the world than bicycle thieves, and the story of a man who discovers his neighbour is just as important and as real as the story of a strike' (ibid.). Fellini's focus on interpersonal ethics continued in his portrait of a petty crook who is an essentially good man in *Il bidone* and then in perhaps his most sophisticated film of the decade, *The Nights of Cabiria*, in which Fellini introduced elements of fantasy, metaphysical quest, spirituality and self-reflexive form which brought neorealism to a point of no return.

Although *The Nights of Cabiria* contains elements of the road narrative, following its protagonist around the city of Rome, the journey which it presents is frustratingly repetitive and circular as the prostitute Cabiria spends the film to-ing and fro-ing monotonously between the desolate suburbs where she lives and the sordid city where she plies her trade. This to-ing and fro-ing is accompanied by a repetitive cycle in Cabiria's disposition as she drifts again and again from hope to disappointment only to end the film in more or less the same position she began. This narrative principle is established in the opening scene as we see an apparently happy romantic couple strolling by a river's edge. Suddenly, the man knocks the woman into the river and runs away with her bag. Presented in long shot, what is happening and who these characters are is not clear – indeed, on several

Fig. 14 Cabiria's long walk home in *The Nights of Cabiria*

occasions in the film Fellini achieves an effect of visual ambiguity which echoes Antonioni's *Cronaca di un amore* – but we presently learn that the woman, rescued from the water and unceremoniously dumped on the bank by a gang of ragamuffin boys, is our 'heroine' and the thief her supposed boyfriend, Giorgio. Held upside down by the legs to get the water out of her lungs, she is introduced to us with all the dignity of an unwanted rag doll and is shunted from romance to indignity, bewilderment to comic humiliation in a rapid switching of register which runs throughout the film.

Cabiria is a protagonist buffeted by a succession of everyday disasters to which her naïve willingness to believe the best of everyone makes her inevitably prone. Like Antonioni and Rossellini, Fellini focuses his film on a female character *in extremis*, but a woman part naïf, part harlot, part saint, rather than a glamorous urban sophisticate. Miserable and alone without Giorgio, Cabiria turns to denial, claiming she fell into the water accidentally, and only acknowledges Giorgio's betrayal under pressure from her worldly-wise best friend, Wanda. Developing on the style of Masina's performance as Gelsomina in *La Strada*, Cabiria is characterised in terms of a fundamental emotional malleability. She shifts repeatedly between pathos and comedy in the manner of a circus clown or mime artist whose performance relies on a non-realist use of exaggerated facial and bodily movement, and her performance is reinforced by an almost constant musical soundtrack which alternates between tearful orchestral strings and the heady rhythms of swing. Cabiria's combination of frustrating naïveté and childlike charm harks back to the American slapstick comedy of the silent era which always fascinated Fellini – the performances of Harold Lloyd and Buster Keaton, but especially of Charlie Chaplin with whose work *The Nights of Cabiria* also shares a thematic interest in the comic buffoon as an icon of poverty and social isolation. Like Chaplin's Little Tramp, Cabiria spends much time wandering around in dejection, a prostitute whose only goal is to find a good man with whom to spend a normal life, but a goal whose repeated anticipation and frustration gives the film what little sense of narrative direction it has: Cabiria expects a kiss from Giorgio but ends up in the river; she hopes to make love to the famous actor Alberto Lazzari but spends the night crashing on his bathroom floor; she allows a hypnotist to convince her she is happily engaged to be married but awakes from her trance a public laughing stock; she falls in love with and agrees to marry Oscar but is robbed by him of every penny and her pride.

Like *Journey to Italy*, Fellini's *The Nights of Cabiria* explores the spiritual poverty of modern society through the figure of an outsider but it goes further in its questioning of neorealism than did Rossellini. If Katherine Joyce suffered from an alienation from the real which she could overcome only by looking at and interacting with the real life of Naples, Cabiria's gullibility suggests that she is too naïvely connected to the real and must achieve distance from it if she is to survive. Fellini questions neorealism by using comedy as a counterweight to its moral piety but, even more importantly, by using two types of space in the city of Rome – one realist, the other fantastic – to articulate her navigation between the mundanity of her daily life and the escapism of her romantic fantasies.

Cabiria's daily routine and, therefore, the film's representational centre of gravity, are located in the poor and marginal quarters of the city which are presented in neorealist fashion through a slowly traveling camera, filming on location with a preference for exterior shots. A series of monotonous and desolate wastelands and back roads drive Cabiria's desire for escape. The opening scene in which she and Giorgio walk by a river presents what at first looks like a pastoral vista, complete with flock of sheep, but is soon revealed to be scrubland on the verge of real estate development, scarred by electricity pylons, building sites, a crane and billboards, and ringed by a distant but approaching skyline of apartments. The scene is aggravated by white noise from a jet plane overhead, a speeding train and the occasional echo of nearby traffic. Cabiria's home, a rudimentary one-room brick hut which stands with a handful of others on empty ground is cut off from the city proper, without amenities or public transport. A threadbare but resilient sense of community prevails among the women and children who gather round open fires at night, the homeless families and tramps whom Cabiria discovers living in caves, and the misfit group of prostitutes, pimps and transvestites with whom she spends her evenings walking the streets. These images situate Cabiria in a social context of poverty and marginality in keeping with neorealism's traditional function of social critique.

However, these realist spaces are contrasted with a variety of fantastic spaces, many involving ornate *mise-en-scène* and filmed indoors at Cinecittà studios. The Piccadilly nightclub where Cabiria dances with the film star Alberto Lazzari and Lazzari's palatial home present an extreme of wealth, glamour and decadent leisure which Cabiria can only dream of. The Piccadilly Club is an exotic space incongruously mixing neon lights, velvet curtains, statues, a piano, 'oriental' dancing and idle rich men in tuxedos drinking in silence. Introduced to its exclusive domain by Lazzari, Cabiria is entirely out of place in it, filled with childlike awe and dancing over-exuberantly in a manner which connotes the un-sophistication of her origins on the street. Lazzari's house is a large, theatrical and somewhat vulgar space containing a fountain, antique furniture, exotic birds, a giant walk-in closet filled with rows of suits, mirrors and rich fabrics, all to the accompaniment of Beethoven's Fifth Symphony. Embarrassed by its opulence, Cabiria lies to Lazzari that she is from 'Rome, Piazza Risorgimento' but is soon reduced to hiding overnight in his bathroom by the arrival of his girlfriend Jessie. The lighting of both the club and Lazzari's home emphasises unnaturally high contrasts of black and white which are underlined by costume as in the case of Lazzari's white tuxedo and Jessie's white fur. These relatively stylised settings point away from neorealism towards Rome's increasingly important role in the late 1950s as an international centre of high fashion and fashion photography. Lazzari's movie stardom and reference to American film producers in Rome evoke a sense of the city's celebrated status as 'Hollywood on the Tiber', capital of a resurgent commercial film industry, epitomised in touristic Hollywood images of Rome such as *Roman Holiday* (William Wyler, 1953) and *Three Coins in the Fountain* (Jean Negulesco, 1954). The Lazzari sequences of *The Nights of Cabiria* therefore not only present a clash of poverty and wealth but also contrast the neorealism of Cabiria's everyday life with the increasing prevalence of escapist and non-realist forms of popular culture in post-war Italy.

Ultimately, Cabiria's encounter with Lazzari leads to disenchantment as the fantastic spaces of the club and his home turn out to be unrewarding. Indeed, variations on this pattern are presented in further encounters with other kinds of fantastic space in the church where Cabiria prays for a miracle to change her life and in the theatre where she falls under the spell of a hypnotist. Signs of religion appear occasionally in Cabiria's habitat – for example, the mysterious procession of people saying the rosary which passes her in the middle of the night – but it is Cabiria's visit with friends to the church of the Madonna del Divino Amore which is central to Fellini's examination of Catholic ritual. Like the scenes with Lazzari, the church sequence is also rich in its *mise-en-scène*, its aerial shots of crowds and tracking shots of hanging crutches, braces and innumerable lights and candles providing a spectacle of religious intensity and devotion. Fellini presents the devotion of his all-too-human characters as a forgiveable trait – indeed, he once expressed the view that 'a certain religious feeling, though broadly interpreted, is necessary' (quoted in Chandler 1995: 294).

At the same time, his presentation of the institutionalised ritual of the Catholic Church recalls the church sequence, and even the fortune-teller sequence, of De Sica's *Bicycle Thieves*. As a crippled old man tries to walk but falls to the floor without his crutches, and as Cabiria and her friends chant in an increasingly desperate frenzy, 'Viva Maria! ... Grazia Madonna!', Fellini's representation of organised religious ritual suggests that the faith in miracles of Rome's ill and dispossessed is little more than folly. Cabiria appears momentarily to recover a religious sense of self but shortly after, more discontent than ever with her life and impatient even with her friends, she gets drunk and stumbles off alone. The fine line between piety and hysteria, pageant and chaos, which the church sequence highlights, is traced further in the magic show (*spettacolo di varietà*) in which Cabiria becomes an actor at a local theatre. The mass spectacle of the hypnotist entrancing willing members of the public in front of a full house echoes the spectacle of organised religion but replaces religious faith with the secular diversion of popular entertainment. Indeed, the hypnotist plays a role not only akin to that of priest but that of the film director, his powers of auto-suggestion commanding a group of men to row an imaginary boat during a heavy storm and deceiving Cabiria into embracing an imaginary ideal man, Oscar, in a field of flowers.

Again and again, in each of these sequences set in fantastic space, the viewer's compassion for Cabiria implicates the viewer, almost but not quite as much as Cabiria herself, in the fantasies of romance and happi-

Fig. 15 Cabiria under the hypnotist's spell in *The Nights of Cabiria*

ness to which she falls prey. The viewer is put through cycles of illusion and disillusion which correspond to hers and which also correspond to the models of neorealist cinema, on the one hand, and of cinema as fantasy and spectacle, on the other, whose relationship is central to the meaning of the film as a whole. In the final phase of the film, which brings this trajectory to a head, Cabiria meets, falls in love with, and is deserted by Oscar Donofrio. This cycle contains the moment of her greatest fantasy and greatest disillusion.

It is Oscar's particular, if warped, skill that he is able to present himself as another naïve soul who shares her willingness to take things at face value. He explains that he was 'touched' by her honesty under the hypnotist's spell and ventures that 'We can all pretend to be cynical and calculating, but when we are faced with purity and candor, the mask of cynicism falls and all that is best in us returns.' Fellini presents Oscar as an antidote to the misleading fantastic encounters which have plagued Cabiria up to this point – indeed, throwing them together in a classic neorealist chance encounter in a crowd. Oscar seduces Cabiria by exploiting her sense of working-class solidarity, emphasising his background as an orphan in wartorn Rome and their shared dream of opening up a modest shop in Grottaferrata on the outskirts of the city. When, in the film's final moments, therefore, Oscar turns out not to be Cabiria's 'angel' but just another traitor who robs her blind, Fellini not only completes his critique of illusionistic and fantastic culture, whether organised religion or popular cinema – he also takes a swipe at neorealism itself. In contrast to De Sica's *Bicycle Thieves* where the thief is a nameless and faceless dramatic mechanism, and where the narrative follows Antonio's recovery from his initial loss, Oscar's theft from Cabiria makes a mockery of the class mobility which her dream of a better life with him presupposed and which was central to the social reformism of neorealist cinema. Fellini closes in on Cabiria's deeply personal anguish which has less to do with the practical issue of her loss of money than it does with her loss of face.

Having cried herself to sleep, Cabiria awakes alone at night in the woods to find life going on despite her despair. Regaining the road, she is surrounded by a group of young partygoers, as if minstrels, and smiles, looking straight at the camera and at the viewer. It is not at all clear what, if anything, she has learned from her trauma. The final shot does not recuperate the film back into an overarching neorealist frame, as Rossellini's conclusion to *Journey to Italy* did by moving from an image of the protagonists to an image of the crowd. Instead, the moment hangs suspended between pathos and comedy and leaves Cabiria on a road whose destination we do not know. The moment is one of affirmation of life, but not necessarily a neorealist one. We might say that *The Nights of Cabiria* works within a neorealist frame but grows out of it in its final moments. Bazin defended the film as neorealist, arguing that it remained 'social in content' if not 'social in intent', but even he recognised that Fellini's symbolism and 'identification with the supernatural' were moving in a new direction (1971a: 87, 89). The flexible definition of neorealism to which Bazin was devoted was strained by the film and the great champion of neorealism had to admit that Cabiria was looking at him in the final shot: 'The invitation is chaste, discreet, and indefinite enough that we can pretend to think that she means to be looking at somebody else. At the same time, though, it is definite and direct enough, too, to remove us quite finally from our role of spectator' (1971a: 92). Arguably, more than any other single image, Cabiria's smile said goodbye to neorealism.

CONCLUSION: LEGACIES OF NEOREALISM

By the end of the 1950s the Italian social, political and cultural landscape had changed substantially. The coming of television in 1956 caused a fall in cinema attendances from a record high of 819m in 1955 to 730m in 1958 and 683m in 1964, a decline which would continue into the 1980s (see Spinazzola 1985: 333). The so-called 'economic miracle' began in earnest around 1958 and continued with a period of unprecedented growth through the early 1960s. Industrial expansion and rising living standards fuelled a proliferation of consumer goods such as radios, cars, refrigerators and televisions and most ordinary Italians enjoyed a new sense of economic security, although the 'economic miracle' would produce its own problems of social inequality which would explode in mass unrest a decade later. As the leading architect Aldo Rossi has explained, the boom replaced the communal ethos of social housing upon which neorealist architecture had been based with a new imperative of corporate and industrial building based upon profit, which turned large areas of many Italian cities into urban-environmental disaster zones overrun by concrete, neon lights and automobiles (1984: 11–12). On the other hand, Italy became renowned for a design culture in which Olivetti, Lambretta, Pinin Farina, Ferragamo and Valentino promoted mass-produced utility, style and private pleasure. As Angelo Restivo has argued, Italy in the 1960s became incorporated in 'the transformation of global capitalism' (2002: 3). Meanwhile, the standing of the PCI, especially among intellectuals, artists and students, was damaged by the 1956 revelations of Stalin's crimes by his successor Nikita Khrushchev and by the Soviet invasion of Hungary (see Duggan 1994: 266; Gundle 2000: 76). These events, combined with the emergence of a New

Left in the 1960s prompted, firstly, the PSI and, then, the PCI into a slow but inexorable rapprochement with the Christian Democrats and other parties. Support for the left remained substantial – around 35–40 per cent right through the 1970s – but new anti-Establishment politics arose and took centre-stage in cinema. These were fuelled by the explosion of a liberal youth-oriented culture facilitated by secularisation in Italian society and by the liberalisation in the attitudes and practices of the Catholic Church brought about by Pope John XXIII from 1958 to 1963.

The combination of these social, political and economic changes was manifest in cinema in 1960 when the tremendous domestic and international success of films such as Antonioni's *L'avventura* and Fellini's *La dolce vita* seemed to announce a new phase of creativity for Italian cinema after the decline of neorealism. As P. Adams Sitney argues, the first neorealist 'vital crisis' of post-war Italian cinema gave way to a second, that of the 1960s art cinema, although neorealism continued to influence all subsequent Italian filmmakers. Of the most important neorealists, Visconti continued to produce great work, Rossellini and De Sica declined, and Antonioni and Fellini were most in tune with the new 1960s generation. Visconti deepened his historical enquiries in *The Leopard* (*Il gattopardo*, 1963) and *The Damned* (La caduta degli dei, 1969) which were visually stylised but foreboding studies of aristocratic or bourgeois social groups in decline. Rossellini, beset by critical and commercial failures, moved into television documentary with *India* (1959) and *La prise de pouvoir par Louis XIV* (1966), making only one further feature film of note, *Il General della Rovere* (1959). De Sica moved back into commercial cinema, having success with romantic comedies such as *Marriage Italian-Style* (*Matrimonio all'italiana*, 1964), starring Marcello Mastroianni and Sophia Loren, although one of his last films, *The Garden of the Finzi-Continis* (*Il Giardino dei Finzi-Contini*, 1970), returned to politically-charged material in dealing with the Italian fascist and Nazi persecution of the Jews. Antonioni reached the peak of his output and acclaim in the 1960s, providing intriguing and disturbing, but increasingly abstract, interrogations of modern urban-industrial society from Ravenna in *Red Desert* (*Il deserto rosso*, 1964) to London in *Blow-Up* (1966) and Los Angeles in *Zabriskie Point* (1969). With *La Dolce Vita* and *8½* (1963), Fellini decisively broke with neorealism, moving into increasingly baroque and often autobiographical examinations of the world of modern Italian movie glamour and celebrity culture, often revolving around characterisations of Rome as a fantastical icon of decadence, corruption and theatrical excess.

By this time, however, the long-lasting and widespread influence of neorealism was in evidence as national cinemas around the world incorporated many of its artistic innovations, examining modernisation, urbanisation and their political and philosophical ramifications in various contexts. Only a few years after *Rome, Open City*, one could see signs of a neorealist influence in the anti-formulaic tendencies and low-budget aesthetics of some American *film noirs* such as *They Live by Night* (Nicholas Ray, 1948) and *The Naked City* (Jules Dassin, 1948). Elsewhere, neorealism fed into movements for social and political reform as in its influence upon Andrzej Wajda's *A Generation* (1955), Satyajit Ray's *Pather Panchali* (1955), Youssef Chahine's *Cairo Station* (1958), Nagisa Oshima's *Cruel Story of Youth* (1960), Glauber Rocha's *Barravento* (1962) and Tomás Gutierrez Alea's *Memories of Underdevelopment* (1968). In documentary film, the Zavattinian model of unmediated interaction of camera and environment was emulated in the *cinéma vérité* of Jean Rouch's *La pyramide humaine* (1960) and the 'direct cinema' of Robert Drew's *Primary* (1960). Its social concern was echoed in portraits of working-class inner-city youth in Britain such as Karel Reisz's *We Are the Lambeth Boys* (1959) and John Schlesinger's *A Kind of Loving* (1962). In France, the *nouvelle vague* internalised many neorealist lessons in their engagement with an everyday Paris, filmed always on location with natural light and highly mobile cameras, and often with an improvisational approach to scripting and shooting. In Italy, the neorealist influence continued in the work of Francesco Rosi and Ermanno Olmi, in Gillo Pontecorvo's *Battle of Algiers* (1966) and, perhaps most of all, in Pier Paolo Pasolini who built upon his first screenwriting credit on Fellini's *The Nights of Cabiria* with *Accattone* (1961), *The Gospel According to Matthew* (1964) and *Theorem* (1968). Many of these filmmakers took for granted neorealism's emphasis on the creative freedom of the director and took inspiration from its belief in cinema as a medium of particular political and poetic potential. Not surprisingly, this was especially evident in the work of filmmakers attracted by neorealism's particular ability to explore relationships of power, engagement and disaffection in the modern city – from *film noir*, which spoke in a dystopian way to processes of urbanisation and modernisation in US society even more intense than those of post-war Italy, to the diverse injustices of the postcolonial city in Chahine, Alea and Pontecorvo.

But 1960s, and then 1970s, cinema also diverged in important ways from all forms of realism, experimenting with spatially- and temporally-disruptive editing, disjointed sound and image, and self-reflexive plays between image and text. These techniques were evident in the work of Jean-Luc Godard, Alain Resnais and Jacques Rivette, and beyond the *nouvelle vague* in the films of Bernardo Bertolucci, Rainer Werner Fassbinder, Wim Wenders and others. If these filmmakers continued neorealism's questioning of modern urban society, and also often worked at odds with mainstream industrial cinema, they intensified the auteurist vision of neorealism, deepened the search for philosophical meaning, accepted ever greater degrees of narrative and visual ambiguity, and focused on internal neuroses and psychoses in new ways.

This experimentation was modernist and anti-realist and was intimately connected with a broad international questioning of post-war society and culture by the 1960s youth generation, and especially by the 'New Left', many of whom poured scorn on the values and actions of their parents during and after World War Two. In Italy, many in the New Left blamed the post-war generation to which the neorealists belonged for not preventing the post-fascist restoration of the bourgeoisie, the Catholic Church and capitalism, arguing that the post-war generation was deeply authoritarian and corrupt in its own ways, if not quite to the same extent as the fascist generation prior to the war. This led to a questioning of the supposed radical break between fascism and the post-war power struggles of the Christian Democrats, Communists and Socialists – a questioning evident in such films as Bertolucci's *The Spider's Strategem* (*La strategia del ragno*, 1970) and the Taviani brothers' *Night of the Shooting Stars* (*La notte di San Lorenzo*, 1982). Among scholars and film enthusiasts, this translated into a questioning of the supposed radical break between fascist-era cinema and neorealism, a questioning which first gained attention in the writings of the so-called 'Gruppo '63' literary avant-garde in the early 1960s and in the important essay by Mario Cannella, 'Ideology and Aesthetic Hypotheses in the Criticism of Neo-Realism', which was first published in the journal *Giovane Critica* in 1966. In an era when the PCI attacked Antonioni for making *Blow-Up* with a Hollywood studio (MGM), it seemed reasonable to doubt the radicalism of the post-war left and, for many, these doubts were confirmed when the PCI agreed to a 'historic compromise' coalition with the PSI and DC in 1973. For many on the New Left, this represented a betrayal of the revolutionary social and political agendas of the 1960s. In 1974, a conference, the Mostra Internazionale del Nuovo Cinema, was held at Pesaro in which leading film scholars of the new generation critiqued neorealism for what they saw as its conservatism rather than its radicalism. Their argument, which became very influential, was that neorealism owed much more to the cinema of the fascist era than was generally admitted and was an effectively conservative aesthetic, like all forms of realism, bound to fail the hopes for revolution which many Italians held in the years immediately after the war.

The problem with this critique of realism, however, was that while it made sense when applied to unadulterated commercial forms of realism such as that of classical Hollywood, or ideologically vulgar forms of realism such as that of fascist Italy or Soviet socialist realism, to apply it to neorealism was overkill. Just as leftists in the late 1940s experienced disillusion with the return of the status quo after the 'liberation', so New Left-ists experienced disillusion with the status quo which they faced in the 1970s and this disillusion informed their critique of neorealism, underestimating the profoundly challenging and controversial impact which many neorealist films exercised on Italian and international society in their day and the great empowering and radicalising influence of neorealism on cinema worldwide.

In the larger historical perspective of the second half of the twentieth century, the flourishing of neorealism in the late 1940s and 1950s, and its subsequent marginalisation by entertainment-oriented cinema such as *neorealismo rosa* and the comedy Italian-style, can be seen either as an important phase in the ongoing struggle between leftist, progressive cinemas and commercial cinema, especially Hollywood, which continues to this day, or as a moment of defeat for leftist, progressive cinemas, another slide downhill for socially-oriented and committed filmmaking towards the abyss of effects-based Hollywood blockbusters which dominate the cinema worldwide and in Italy today. From the point of view of readers in the present-day, the ideological differences exposed in Italy by such films as *Bicycle Thieves* in 1948 and Fellini's *La Strada* in 1954, which seemed gargantuan at the time and generated arguments of real moral and political urgency, may seem relatively incidental. Such neorealist films, seen as worlds apart then, seem relatively close today in their visual style, their ethics, and their politics, and stand in obvious contrast to the dominant cinematic *gestalt* of the early twenty-first century.

As many commentators since the 1970s have attested, 'postmodernism' has ushered in a film culture in which notions of 'the real' have played precious little part. Italian cinema, like most other European cinemas, has struggled to replicate either the commercial success or the consistent artistic excellence of the post-war period. Hollywood cinema has expanded and deepened its penetration on a diet composed primarily of high-concept extravanganzas and, recently, new digital technologies have blurred the distinctions between cinema itself and other forms of visual and textual culture in a multimedia environment. In all of this, the notion of representing 'the real' – real society, real cities, real people – has become more and more compromised and, indeed, commodified. In this cultural climate, perhaps the time is right to reclaim the real for its radical potential.

BIBLIOGRAPHY

Works cited

Alicata, Mario and Giuseppe De Santis (1979 [1941]) 'Truth and Poetry: Verga and the Italian Cinema', in David Overbey (ed.) *Springtime in Italy: A Reader in Neorealism*. Hamden, CT: Archon Books, 131–8.

Antonioni, Michelangelo (1940a) 'Inaugurazione', *Cinema*, 10 September.

____ (1940b) 'La sorpresa veneziana', *Cinema*, 25 September.

____ (1996) *The Architecture of Vision: Writings and Interviews on Cinema*, edited by Carlo di Carlo, Giorgio Tinazzi and Marga Cottino-Jones, New York: Marsilio Publishers.

Aprà, Adriano and Patrizia Pistagnesi (eds) (1979) *The Fabulous Thirties: Italian Cinema, 1929–1944*, Milan: Electa International.

Aristarco, Guido (1943) Review of *Ossessione*, *Corriere Padano*, 8 June.

____ (ed.) (1950) *L'arte del film*. Milan: Bompiani.

____ (1951) *Storia delle teoriche del film*. Turin: Einaudi.

____ (1955a) Review of *Senso*, *Cinema nuovo*, 52, 10 February.

____ (1955b) 'È realismo', *Cinema nuovo*, 55, 21 March.

____ (1996) *Il cinema fascista: Il prima e il dopo*. Bari: Dedalo.

Armes, Roy (1971) *Patterns of Realism: A Study of Italian Neo-Realism*. Cranbury, NJ: A. S. Barnes.

Aumont, Jacques, Alain Bergala, Michel Marie and Marc Vernet (1999) *Aesthetics of Film*. Austin: University of Texas Press.

Ayfre, Amedée (1985 [1952]) 'Neo-Realism and Phenomenology', in Jim Hillier (ed.) *Cahiers du cinéma: Volume One, The 1950s: Neorealism, Hollywood, New Wave*. Cambridge, MA: Harvard University Press, 182–7.

Barber, Stephen (1995) *Fragments of the European City*. Reaktion Books.

Bazin, André (1971a) *What is Cinema, vol. 1*, trans. Hugh Gray. Berkeley: University of California Press.

_____ (1971b) *What is Cinema, vol. 2*, trans. Hugh Gray. Berkeley: University of California Press.

_____ (1985 [1952]) 'La foi qui sauve: Cannes 1952', in Jim Hillier (ed.) *Cahiers du cinéma: Volume One, The 1950s: Neorealism, Hollywood, New Wave*. Cambridge, MA: Harvard University Press, 179–81.

Benjamin, Walter and Asja Lacis (1986) 'Naples', in *Reflections*. New York: Schocken, 163–76.

Berman, Marshall (1983) *All that is Solid Melts into Air*. London and New York: Verso.

Bondanella, Peter (1993) *The Films of Roberto Rossellini*. Cambridge and New York: Cambridge University Press.

_____ (2001) *Italian Cinema from Neorealism to the Present*. New York: Continuum.

Bordwell, David (1993) *Narration in the Fiction Film*. London and New York: Routledge.

Bown, Matthew C. (1998) *Socialist Realist Painting*. New Haven and London: Yale University Press.

Brunetta, Gian Piero (1995) *Cent'anni di cinema italiano*. Rome-Bari: Laterza.

_____ (ed.) (1996) *Identità italiana e identità europea nel cinema italiano*. Turin: Edizioni della Fondazione Giovanni Agnelli.

_____ (2001) *Storia del cinema italiano: Il cinema del regime, 1929–1945*. Rome: Riuniti.

Brunette, Peter (1998) *The Films of Michelangelo Antonioni*. New York: Cambridge University Press.

Bruno, Giuliana (1993) *Streetwalking on a Ruined Map: Cultural Theory and the City Films of Elvira Notari*. Princeton: Princeton University Press.

_____ (1997) 'City Views: The Voyage of Film Images', in David B. Clarke (ed.) *The Cinematic City*. London and New York: Routledge, 46–58.

Burgin, Victor (1998) 'The City in Pieces', in Laura Marcus and Lynda Nead (eds) *The Actuality of Walter Benjamin*. London: Lawrence and Wishart.

Cannella, Mario (1973 [1966]), 'Ideology and Aesthetic Hypotheses in the Criticism of Neo-Realism', *Screen*, Winter, 14, 4, 5–60.

Casetti, Francesco (1999) *Theories of Cinema, 1945–1995*. Austin: University of Texas Press.

Chandler, Charlotte (1995) *I, Fellini*. New York: Random House.

Charney, Leo and Vanessa R. Schwartz (eds) (1995) *Cinema and the Invention of Modern Life*. Berkeley and Los Angeles: University of California Press.

Chatman, Seymour (1985) *Antonioni, or the Surface of the World*. Berkeley: University of California Press.

Chiarini, Luigi (1979 [1950]) 'A Discourse on Neo-Realism', in David Overbey (ed.) *Springtime in Italy: A Reader in Neorealism*. Hamden, CT: Archon Books, 138–68.

Clark, Martin (1996) *Modern Italy, 1871–1995*. London and New York: Longman.

Croce, Benedetto (1929) *A History of Italy, 1871–1915*, trans. Cecilia M. Ady. Oxford: The Clarendon Press.

Crowther, Bosley (1946) 'The Screen: How Italy Resisted', *New York Times*, 26 February, 32.

Dalle Vacche, Angela (1992) *The Body in the Mirror: Shapes of History in Italian Cinema*. Princeton: Princeton University Press.

Della Volpe, Galvano (1972 [1954]) *Verosimile filmico e altri scritti di estetica*, in Edoardo Bruno (ed.) *Teorie e prassi del cinema in Italia, 1950–1970*. Milan: Mazzotta, 15.

De Matteis, Giuseppe, Piero Bonavero and Fabio Sforzi (1999) *The Italian Urban System: Towards European Integration*, Brookfield, VT: Ashgate.

De Santis, Giuseppe (1979a [1941]) 'Towards an Italian Landscape', in David Overbey (ed.) *Springtime in Italy: A Reader in Neorealism*. Hamden, CT: Archon Books, 125–9.

De Santis, Giuseppe, with Pietro Germi and Luchino Visconti (1979b [1946]) 'In Defense of the Italian Cinema', in David Overbey (ed.) *Springtime in Italy: A Reader in Neorealism*. Hamden, CT: Archon Books, 215–20.

De Sica, Vittorio (1969) 'How I Direct My Films', in *Miracle in Milan*. Baltimore, MD: Penguin.

_____ (1979 [1948]) 'Why *Ladri di Biciclette*?', in David Overbey (ed.) *Springtime in Italy: A Reader in Neorealism*. Hamden, CT: Archon Books, 87–8.

Debreczeni, François (1964) 'Origines et évolution du néoréalisme', in *Le Néoréalisme Italien: bilan de la critique*, Études cinématographiques, nos. 32–35. Paris: Lettres modernes, 20–54.

Dimendberg, Edward (2004) *Film Noir and the Spaces of Modernity*. Cambridge, MA: Harvard University Press.

Donald, James (1999) *Imagining the Modern City*. Athlone Press.

Duggan, Christopher (1994) *A Concise History of Italy*. Cambridge: Cambridge University Press.

Etlin, Richard A. (1990) *Modernism in Italian Architecture, 1890–1940*. Cambridge, MA: MIT Press.

Farassino, Alberto (1998) 'Historie et géographie du néoréalisme', in Sergio Toffetti (ed.) *Un'Altra Italia: Pour une histoire du cinéma italien*. Paris: Cinémathèque française and Milan: Mazzotta, 72–9.

Fer, Briony, David Batchelor and Paul Wood (1993) *Realism, Rationalism, Surrealism: Art between the Wars*. New Haven and London: Yale University Press.

Ferrara, Giuseppe (1963) *Luchino Visconti*. Paris: Éditions Seghers.

Forgacs, David (1990) *Italian Culture in the Industrial Era, 1880–1980: Cultural Industries, Politics, and the Public*. Manchester: University of Manchester Press.

Fried, Robert C. (1973) *Planning the Eternal City*. New Haven and London: Yale University Press.

Gallagher, Tag (1998) *The Adventures of Roberto Rossellini: His Life and Films*. New York: Da Capo Press.

Gaughan, Martin (2003) 'Ruttmann's Berlin: Filming in a "Hollow Space"', in Mark Shiel and Tony Fitzmaurice (eds) *Screening the City*. London and New York: Verso, 41–57.

Gramsci, Antonio (1971) *Selections from the Prison Notebooks of Antonio Gramsci*, edited and translated by Quintin Hoare and Geoffrey Nowell Smith. London: Lawrence and Wishart.

Gregotti, Vittorio (1968) *New Directions in Italian Architecture*, trans. Giuseppina Salvadori. London: Studio Vista.

Gundle, Stephen (2000) *Between Hollywood and Moscow: The Italian Communists and the Challenge of Mass Culture, 1943–1991*. Durham, NC: Duke University Press.

Hansen, Miriam Bratu (1997) 'Introduction' to Siegfried Kracauer, *Theory of Film: The Redemption of Physical Reality*. Princeton: Princeton University Press, vii–xlv.

Hay, James (1987) *Popular Film Culture in Fascist Italy: The Passing of the Rex*. Bloomington: University of Indiana Press.

Kracauer, Siegfried (1997 [1960]) *Theory of Film: The Redemption of Physical Reality*. Princeton: Princeton University Press.

Landy, Marcia (2000) *Italian Film*. New York: Cambridge University Press.

Leprohon, Pierre (1972) *The Italian Cinema*, trans. Roger Greaves and Oliver Stallybrass. London: Secker and Warburg.

Liehm, Mira (1984) *Passion and Defiance: Film in Italy from 1942 to the Present*. Berkeley: University of California Press.

Lizzani, Carlo (1948) 'Per una difesa attiva del cinema popolare', *Rinascita*, 5, 2, 91.

_____ (1953) *Il cinema italiano*. Florence: Parenti.

MacCabe, Colin (1974) 'Realism and the Cinema: Notes on Some Brechtian Theses', *Screen*, 15, 2, 7–27.

Mafai, Miriam (2001) 'Roma, dal 18 aprile alla dolce vita', in Maurizio Fagiolo Dell'Arco and Claudi Terenzi (eds) *Arte, cronaca e cultura dal neorealismo alla dolce vita*, Milan: Skira, 4–21.

Marinetti, Filippo Tommasi (1993 [1909]) 'The Foundation and Manifesto of Futurism', in Charles Harrison and Paul Wood (eds) *Art in Theory, 1900–1990: An Anthology of Changing Ideas*. Oxford and Cambridge, MA: Blackwell, 145–9.

Messenger, Charles (1989) *The Chronological Atlas of World War Two*. London and New York: Macmillan.

Miccichè, Lino (ed.) (1999) *Il neorealismo cinematografico italiano* (second edition). Venice: Marsilio.

Michalczyk, John J. (1986) *The Italian Political Filmmakers*. Cranbury, NJ and

London: Associated University Presses.

Mulvey, Laura (2000) 'Vesuvian Topographies: The Eruption of the Past in *Journey to Italy*', in David Forgacs, Sarah Lutton and Geoffrey Nowell-Smith (eds) *Roberto Rossellini: Magician of the Real*. London: British Film Institute, 95–111.

Nowell-Smith, Geoffrey (2003) *Luchino Visconti* (third edition). London: British Film Institute.

Pasolini, Pier Paolo (1965) *Le notti di Cabiria*. Modena: Capelli.

Pica, Agnoldomenico (1959) *Recent Italian Architecure*. Milan: Edizioni del Milone.

Pitkin, Donald S. (1993) 'Italian Urbanscape: Intersection of Private and Public', in Robert Rotenberg and Gary McDonogh (eds) *The Cultural Meaning of Urban Space*, Westport, CT: Bergin and Garvey, 95–102.

Quaglietti, Lorenzo (1974) *Il cinema italiano del dopoguerra*. Rome: Mostra Internazionale del Nuovo cinema.

____ (1980) *Storia economico-politica del cinema italiano, 1945–1980*. Rome: Riuniti.

Quaresima, Lenoardo (1996) 'Parigi ci appartiene? Modelli francesi nel cinema italiano del dopoguerra', in Gian Piero Brunetta (ed.) *Identità italiana e identità europea nel cinema italiano*. Turin: Edizioni della Fondazione Giovanni Agnelli, 441–68.

Restivo, Angelo (2002) *The Cinema of Economic Miracles: Visuality and Modernisation in the Italian Art Film*. Durham, NC and London: Duke University Press.

Rivette, Jacques (1985 [1955]) 'Letter on Rossellini', in Jim Hillier (ed.) *Cahiers du cinéma: Volume One, The 1950s: Neorealism, Hollywood, New Wave*. Cambridge, MA: Harvard University Press, 192–202.

Rohmer, Eric (1985 [1955]) 'The Land of Miracles', in Jim Hillier (ed.) *Cahiers du cinéma: Volume One, The 1950s: Neorealism, Hollywood, New Wave*. Cambridge, MA: Harvard University Press, 205–8.

Rossellini, Roberto (1946) 'Roberto Rossellini, réalisateur de *Rome ville ouverte*, expose ses conceptions', interview in *Le Figaro*, 20 November.

____ (1979 [1955]) 'Ten Years of Cinema', in David Overbey (1979) *Springtime in Italy: A Reader in Neorealism*. Hamden, CT: Archon Books, 93–113.

____ (1985 [1954]) interview with Eric Rohmer and François Truffaut, in Jim Hillier (ed.) *Cahiers du cinéma: Volume One, The 1950s: Neorealism, Hollywood, New Wave*. Cambridge, MA: Harvard University Press, 209–12.

Rossi, Aldo (1984) *Three Cities: Perugia, Milano, Mantova*. Milan: Electa.

Rowe, Peter G. (1997) *Civic Realism*. Cambridge, MA: MIT Press.

Samuels, Charles Thomas (1987) *Encountering Directors* (second edition). New York: Da Capo Press.

Servadio, Gaia (1980) *Luchino Visconti*, trans. Paola Campioli. Milan: Mondadori.

Sforzi, Fabio, Piero Bonavero and Giuseppe De Matteis (1999) *The Italian Urban*

System: Towards European Integration. Brookfield, VT: Ashgate.

Sitney, P. Adams (1995) *Vital Crises in Italian Cinema: Iconography, Stylistics, Politics*. Austin: University of Texas Press.

Sorlin, Pierre (1996) *Italian National Cinema, 1896–1996*. London and New York: Routledge.

Spinazzola, Vittorio (1985) *Cinema e pubblico: Lo spetaccolo filmico in Italia, 1945–1965*. Rome: Bulzoni.

Strathausen, Carsten (2003) 'Uncanny Space: The City in Ruttmann and Vertov', in Mark Shiel and Tony Fitzmaurice (eds) *Screening the City*. London and New York: Verso, 15–40.

Tafuri, Manfredo (1989) *History of Italian Architecture, 1944–1985*, trans Jessica Levine. Cambridge, MA: MIT Press.

Vitti, Antonio (1996) *Giuseppe de Santis and Postwar Italian Cinema*. Toronto: University of Toronto Press.

Vittorini, Elio (1979 [1947]) 'Politics and Culture: A Letter to Togliatti', in David Overbey (ed.) *Springtime in Italy: A Reader in Neorealism*. Hamden, CT: Archon Books, 41–66.

Wagstaff, Christopher (1996) 'Il cinema italiano nel mercato internazionale', in Gian Piero Brunetta (ed.) *Identità italiana e identità europea nel cinema italiano*. Turin: Edizioni della Fondazione Giovanni Agnelli, 141–72.

Ward, Janet (2001) *Weimar Surfaces: Urban Visual Culture in 1920s Germany*. University of California Press.

Zavattini, Cesare (1970) *Zavattini: Sequences from a Cinematic Life*, trans. William Weaver. Englewood Cliffs, NJ: Prentice-Hall.

_____ (1979a [1952]) 'Some Ideas on the Cinema', included in 'A Thesis on Neo-Realism', in David Overbey (ed.) *Springtime in Italy: A Reader in Neorealism*. Hamden, CT: Archon Books, 67–78.

_____ (1979b) *Neorealismo ecc*, edited by Mini Argentieri. Milan: Bompiani.

Secondary reading

Ades, Dawn (ed.) (1995) *Art and Power: Europe under the Dictators, 1930-45*. London: Thames and Hudson, in association with the Hayward Gallery.

Antonioni, Michelangelo (1986) *That Bowling Alley on the Tiber: Tales of a Director*. New York: Oxford University Press.

Aprà, Adriano and Jean A. Gili (1994) *Naples et le cinéma*. Paris: Centre Georges Pompidou.

Aristarco, Guido (1965) *Il Dissolvimento della ragione: Discorso sul cinema*. Milan: Feltrinelli.

_____ (1972) *Marx, le cinéma et la critique de film*, trans. Barthélemy Amengual, with preface by George Lukacs, Études cinématographiques, nos 88–92, Lettres modernes. Minard: Paris.

_____ (1980) *Neorealismo e Nuova Critica Cinematografica, Cinema-tografia e Vita Nazionale: Tra Rottura e Tradizioni*. Florence: Nuova Guaraldi.

Arrowsmith, William (1995) *Antonioni: A Critical Study*. New York: Oxford University Press.

Bacon, Henry (1998) *Visconti: Explorations of Beauty and Decay*. Cambridge: Cambridge University Press.

Barbaro, Umberto (1951) 'Importanza del realismo', *Filmcritica*, 4, 113–17.

_____ (1960) *Il Film*. Rome: Editori Riuniti.

_____ (1962) *Servitù e grandezza del cinema*. Rome: Editori Riuniti.

Benevolo, Leonardo (1993) *The European City*, trans. Carl Ipsen, Oxford: Blackwell

Ben-Ghiat, Ruth (2001) *Fascist Modernities: Italy, 1922–1945*. Berkeley and London: University of California Press.

Bernardini, Aldo and Jean A. Gili (1986) *Le Cinéma italien de La prise de Rome (1905) à Rome ville ouverte (1945)*. Paris: Centre Georges Pompidou.

_____ (eds) (1990) *Cesare Zavattini*. Paris: Éditions du Centre Pompidou/Bologna: Edizioni di Regione Emilia-Romagna.

Bertolucci, Bernardo (1987) *Bertolucci by Bertolucci*, trans. Donald Ranvaud, London: Plexus.

_____ (2000) *Bernardo Bertolucci: Interviews*, edited by Fabien S. Gerard, T. Jefferson Kline and Bruce Sklarew. Jackson: Mississippi University Press.

Bocchi, Francesca, Manuela Ghizzoni and Rosa Smurra (2002) *Storia delle città italiane: dal Tardoantico al primo Rinascimento*, Turin: UTET Libreria.

Bondanella, Peter (ed.) (1978) *Federico Fellini: Essays in Criticism*. Oxford: Oxford University Press.

_____ (1987) *The Eternal City: Roman Images in the Modern World*. Chapel Hill: University of North Carolina Press.

_____ (1992) *The Cinema of Federico Fellini*. Princeton: Princeton University Press.

_____ (2001) *The Films of Federico Fellini*. New York: Cambridge University Press.

Bondanella, Peter and Cristina Degli-Esposti (1993) *Perspectives on Federico Fellini*. New York: G. K. Hall/Macmillan.

Bondanella, Peter and Manuela Gieri (eds) (1987) *Federico Fellini: Director*. New Brunswick, NJ: Rutgers University Press.

Borden, Iain (1996) *Strangely Familiar: Narratives of Architecture in the City*. London: Routledge.

Braudy, Leo Braudy and Morris Dickstein (1978) *Great Film Directors: A Critical Anthology*. New York: Oxford University Press.

Brunetta, Gian Piero (1987) *Cinema storia resistenza: 1944–1985*. Milan: Franco Angeli.

Brunette, Peter (1987) *Roberto Rossellini*. New York: Oxford University Press.

Bruno, Giuliana and Maria Nadotti (eds) (1988) *Offscreen: Women and Film in Italy*. London: Routledge.

Buache, Freddy (1992) *Le cinéma italien: 1945–1990*. Lausanne: L'Age d'Homme.

Burke, Frank (1996) *Fellini's Films: From Postwar to Postmodern*. New York: Twayne.

Cameron, Ian (1968) *Antonioni*. London: Studio Vista.

Caramel, Luciano (2001) *Realismi: Arti figurative, letteratura e cinema in Italia dal 1943 al 1953*. Milan: Electa.

Celant, Germano (ed.) (1994) *The Italian Metamorphosis, 1943–1968*. New York: Guggenheim Museum Publications/Harry N. Abrams.

Chiarini, Luigi (1954) *Il film nella battaglia delle idee*. Milan and Rome: Fratelli Boca.

_____ (1959) 'Umberto Barbaro, uomo e maestro', *Bianco e nero*, 20, 6, 13–29.

_____ (1962) *Arte e tecnica del film*. Bari: Laterza.

Ciacci, Leonardo (2001) *Progetti di città sullo schermo: Il cinema degli urbanisti*. Venice: Marsilio.

Cités-Cinés (1987) La Villette: Éditions Ramsay

Cladel, Gérard, Kristian Feigelson, Jean-Michel Gévaudan, Christian Landais and Daniel Sauvaget (2001) *Le Cinéma dans la cité*. Paris: Éditions du Félin.

Clarke, David B. (ed.) (1997) *The Cinematic City*. New York and London: Routledge.

Constantini, Constanza (1995) *Fellini on Fellini*. London: Faber.

Curl, James Stevens (1970) *European Cities and Society*. London: Leonard Hill.

Curle, Howard and Stephen Snyder (eds) (2000) *Vittorio de Sica: Contemporary Perspectives*. Toronto: University of Toronto Press.

Darretta, John (1983) *Vittorio De Sica: A Guide to References and Resources*. Boston: G. K. Hall.

De Grazia, Victoria (1981) *The Culture of Consent: Mass Organization of Leisure in Fascist Italy*. Cambridge and New York: Cambridge University Press.

_____ (1992) *How Fascism Ruled Women*. Berkeley: University of California Press.

Dell'Arco, Maurizio Fagiolo and Claudi Terenzi (eds) (2001) *Arte, cronaca e cultura dal neorealismo alla dolce vita*. Milan: Skira.

Dethier, Jean and Alain Guiheux (1994) *La Ville: Art et architecture en Europe, 1870–1993*. Paris: Centre Georges Pompidou.

Farassino, Alberto (ed.) (1989) *Neorealismo: Cinema italiano, 1945–1949*, Torino: EDT.

Fellini, Federico (1988) *Comments on Film*. Fresno: California State College at Fresno Press.

_____ (1996) *Fellini on Fellini*, trans. Isabel Quigley. New York: Da Capo Press.

Forgacs, David (2000) *Rome Open City*. London: British Film Institute.

Georgakas, Dan and Lenny Rubenstein (eds) (1983) *The Cinéaste Interviews on the Art and Politics of the Cinema*. Chicago: Lake View Press.

Greene, Naomi (1990) *Pier Paolo Pasolini: Cinema as Heresy*. Princeton: Princeton University Press.

Hovald, Patrice G. (1959) *Neo-realisme italien et ses créateurs*. Paris: Cerf.

Ingold, Alice (2003) *Négocier la ville: Projet urbaine, société et fascisme à Milan*. Paris and Rome: Éditions de l'École des hautes études en sciences sociales/ Éditions Française de Rome.

Insolera, Italo (1993) *Roma Moderna: Un secolo di storia urbanistica, 1870–1970*. Rome: Einaudi.

Landy, Marcia (1986) *Fascism in Film: The Italian Commercial Cinema, 1931–1943*, Princeton: Princeton University Press.

_____ (1994) *Film, Politics, and Gramsci*. Minneapolis: University of Minnesota Press.

_____ (1998) *The Folklore of Consensus: Theatricality in the Italian Cinema, 1930– 1943*. Albany: State University of New York Press.

Laura, Ernesto (1979) 'A proposito di generi: il film comico', in Riccardo Redi (ed.) *Cinema italiano sotto il fascismo*. Venice: Marsilio, 117–28.

Licata, Antonella and Elisa Mariani-Travi (2000) *La città e il cinema*. Universale di architettura, Rome: Testo e immagine.

Lucanio, Patrick (1994) *With Fire and Sword: Italian Spectacles on American Screens, 1958–68*. London and Metuchen, NJ: Scarecrow Press.

Lyons, Robert J. (1976) *Michelangelo Antonioni's Neorealism: A World View*. New York: Arno Press.

Mancini, Elaine (1985) *Struggles of the Italian Film Industry During Fascism, 1930–1935*. Ann Arbor: UMI Research Press.

Marcus, Laura and Lynda Nead (eds) (1998) *The Actuality of Walter Benjamin*. London: Lawrence and Wishart.

Marcus, Millicent (1986) *Italian Cinema in the Light of Neorealism*. Princeton: Princeton University Press.

_____ (1993) *Filmmaking by the Book: Italian Cinema and Literary Adaptation*. Baltimore: Johns Hopkins University Press.

_____ (2001) *Toward a New Italian Cinema: Emerging from the Shadows of the Video Age*. Baltimore: Johns Hopkins University Press.

Margulies, Ivone (2003) 'Exemplary Bodies: Reenactment in Love in the City, Sons, and Close-Up', in Ivone Margulies (ed.) *Rites of Realism: Essays on Corporeal Cinema*. Durham and London: Duke University Press, 217–44.

Masi, Stefano (1982) *Giuseppe De Santis*. Florence: La nuova Italia.

Mazierska, Ewa and Laura Rascaroli (2003) *From Moscow to Madrid: Postmodern Cities, European Cinema*. London and New York: I. B. Tauris.

Meller, Helen (2001) *European Cities, 1890–1930s: History, Culture, and the Built Environment*. Chichester and New York: John Wiley & Sons.

Miccichè, Lino (1992) *De Sica: autore, regista, attore*. Venice: Marsilio.

Micchichè, Lino (1990) *Visconti e il neorealismo: Ossessione, La terra trema, Bellissima*. Venice: Marsilio.

Mida, Massimo and Lorenzo Quaglietti (1980) *Dai telefoni bianchi al neorealismo*.

Rome-Bari: Laterza.

Nowell-Smith, Geoffrey (ed.) (1996a) *The Oxford History of World Cinema*. Oxford: Oxford University Press.

Nowell-Smith, Geoffrey with James Hay and Gianni Volpe (1996b) *The Companion to Italian cinema*. London: British Film Institute.

Nuzzi, Paolo (1997) *De Sica & Zavattini: parliamo tanto di noi*. Roma: Editori riuniti.

Pacifici, Sergio (1962) *A Guide to Contemporary Italian Literature: From Futurism to Neorealism*. Cleveland: World Publishing.

Pasolini, Pier Paolo (1989) *Pier Paolo Pasolini: A Cinema of Poetry*, edited by Laura Betti and Lodovico Gambara Thovazzi. Rome: Associazione 'Fondo Pier Paolo Pasolini', Ente autonomo gestione cinema.

Penz, François and Maureen Thomas (1997) *Cinema and Architecture*. London: British Film Institute.

Re, Lucia (1990) *Calvino and the Age of Neorealism: Fables of Estrangement*. Stanford: Stanford University Press.

Reich, Jacqueline and Piero Garofalo (2002) *Re-Viewing Fascism: Italian Cinema, 1922–1943*. Bloomington: Indiana University Press.

Rocchio, Vincent F. (1999) *Cinema of Anxiety: A Psychoanalysis of Italian Neorealism*. Austin: University of Texas Press.

Rohdie, Sam (1990) *Antonioni*. London: British Film Institute.

_____ (1995) *The Passion of Pier Paolo Pasolini*. Bloomington: University of Indiana Press.

Rondolino, Gianni (1974) *Roberto Rossellini*. Florence: La Nuova Italia.

Rosenstone, Robert A. (ed.) (1995) *Revisioning History: Film and the Construction of a New Past*. Princeton: Princeton University Press.

Rosetti, Franco (1954) 'La provincia nell'ultimo cinema italiano', *Bianco e nero*, 15, 11–12, 120–5.

Rossellini, Roberto (1992) *My Method: Writings and Interviews*. New York: Marsilio.

Rumble, Patrick and Bart Testa (eds) (1994) *Pier Paolo Pasolini: Contemporary Perspectives*. Toronto: University of Toronto Press.

Schifano, Laurence (1990) *Luchino Visconti: The Flames of Passion*. London: Collins.

Schumacher, Thomas L. (1991) *Surface and Symbol: Giuseppe Terragni and the Architecture of Italian Rationalism*. New York: Princeton Architectural Press.

Shiel, Mark and Tony Fitzmaurice (eds) (2001) *Cinema and the City: Film and Urban Societies in a Global Context*. Oxford and New York: Blackwell.

Snyder, Stephen (1980) *Pier Paolo Pasolini*. Boston: Twayne.

Soldati, Mario (1991) *Mario Soldati: la scrittura e lo sguardo*. Turin: Lindau: Museo nazionale del cinema.

Sorlin, Pierre (1991) *European Cinemas, European Societies, 1939–1990*. New

York: Routledge.

Steele, Valerie (1994) 'Italian Fashion and America', in Germano Celant (ed.) *The Italian Metamorphosis, 1943–1968*. New York: Guggenheim Museum Publications/Harry N. Abrams, 496–506.

Sterling, Monica (1979) *A Screen of Time: A Study of Luchino Visconti*. New York: Harcourt Brace Jovanovich.

Tisdall, Caroline and Angelo Bozzolla (1978) *Futurism*. New York and Toronto: Oxford University Press.

Tonetti, Claretta (1983) *Luchino Visconti*. Boston: Twayne.

Tornabuoni, Lietta (ed.) (1995) *Federico Fellini*. New York: Rizzoli/St Martin's Press.

Viano, Maurizio (1993) *A Certain Realism: Making Use of Pasolini's Film Theory and Practice*. Berkeley: University of California Press.

Waley, Daniel (1988) *The Italian City Republics*. London and New York: Longman.

Willemen, Paul (1977) *Pier Paolo Pasolini*. London: British Film Institute.

Williams, Christopher (1980) *Realism and the Cinema: A Reader*. London: Routledge & Kegan Paul.

Wollen, Peter (1998) *Signs and Meaning in the Cinema* (second edition). London: British Film Institute.

INDEX

80, 123, 125
Puccini, Gianni 38, 44, 46, 54, 82
Pudovkin, Vsevolod 21, 37

Quaroni, Ludovico 2, 76–7

Ravenna 123
Ray, Nicholas 124
Ray, Satyajit 124
Reisz, Karel 124
Renoir, Jean 9, 17–18, 22, 28, 30, 37
Resnais, Alain 125
Restivo, Angelo 66, 110, 122
Ridolfi, Mario 1–2, 72, 76–7
Riefenstahl, Leni 28
Riganti, Franco 31
Risorgimento 15, 24, 93, 118
Rivera, Diego 28
Rivette, Jacques 112, 125
Rocha, Glauber 124
Rogers, Ernesto 74
Rohmer, Eric 112
Rosi, Francesco 88, 124
Rossellini, Roberto 1, 3–4, 11, 13–14,
    18, 21, 23, 30–5, 40, 45, 47–52,
    54, 64, 67, 69–70, 73, 76, 81–2,
    94–6, 98, 100, 104–13, 116–17,
    120, 123
Rossi, Aldo 122
Rotha, Paul 68
Rouch, Jean 124
Rowe, Peter 75–6
Ruttmann, Walter 28

Sadoul, Georges 20
Sanders, George 106
Sant'Elia, Antonio 70
Sartre, Jean-Paul 89
Schlesinger, John 124
Seaton, George 68
Selznick, David O. 56
Serafin, Enzo 107

Serandrei, Mario 8
Simonelli, Giorgio 24
Sitney, P. Adams 7–8, 51, 53, 80, 123
social realism 2, 27
socialist realism 62, 89, 91, 126
Soldati, Mario 19, 22, 29–30
Sorlin, Pierre 4–5, 18, 26
Spanish Civil War 21, 29, 40
Staiola, Enzo 56
Stalin, Joseph 62, 81, 122
Steinbeck, John 19
Stone, Rear Admiral Emery W. 85
Strand, Paul 28

Tafuri, Manfredo 75–7, 79
Taviani, Paolo 125
Taviani, Vittorio 125
Togliatti, Palmiro 84
Tonti, Aldo 3
Tourneur, Jacques 68

Verga, Giovanni 12, 29–31, 82
Vergano, Aldo 3, 11, 81, 83
Vertov, Dziga 68, 90
Vidor, King 18, 30
Visconti, Luchino 1, 3–4, 9, 11–15,
    18–20, 26, 30–1, 36–41, 43, 46–7,
    63–4, 67, 74, 80–6, 89, 93–4, 96,
    98, 106, 123
Vittorini, Elio 2, 12, 19, 46, 80–1

Wajda, Andrzej 124
Wenders, Wim 125
'white telephone' films 25, 38, 49
Wiene, Robert 27
Wyler, William 18, 118

Zampa, Luigi 3, 21, 64, 86, 114
Zavattini, Cesare 3–4, 12–15, 26,
    30–1, 34, 54–5, 89–94, 113, 124
Zevi, Bruno 74